...ler  Monica A. Adley   Charles Aenlle   John Agnew   Gena Aiello   Gil Aiken   John W. Akamatsu   Lydia Aldredge
Carrie A. Anderson   Divina G. Anderson   Elizabeth L. Anderson   Eric L. Anderson   Eric W. Anderson   Kjell M. Anderson
...bio Arevalo   Denise E. Arluck   Edward Armstrong   Guiula Aronowitz   Robert Asahara   Kathryn Atcher   Alan Atkinson
   G. Lloyd Baker   David Balas   Brenda Ball   Laurens D. Banker   Rodney S. Bannon   Bradley S. Barbee   Bridgett Barker
...tes   M. Christine Bates   Debra Battle   Judith Bauer   Elisabeth Baumberger   Scott Baumberger   Erin Baumstark
Cheryl Bentley   Lisa Berenson Repyak   W. Randy Berg   Bruce Bergman   Kristin Bergman   Kevin Berry   John Berryman
...iggs   Matthew J. Billerbeck   Andre B. Bilokur   Andre Binder   John Bisschop   Cur...   ...hen Blackstone
   Daniel R. Bogh   James Bohannon   John Bohn   Christopher A. Boldt   Cur...   ...   ...n   Randi Bosley
Michael Braden   Amy Bradford   Karen Braitmayer   Bonnie Brakken   L. Car...   ...eau   Jan Bredal
David F. Brown   Helen W. Brown   Scott R. Brown   Ryan R. Bruce   Donna Bu...   ...   C. Don Bullard
...zabeth L. Buxton   Jennifer Byers   Brigid A. Byrne   Lori Byrne   Medardo T. Cadiz   Donald A. Caffrey   Tara Cahn
...rlander   Jennifer Carlisle   Chris Carlson   Christian Carlson   Kathleen J. Carlson   Trina Carlson   William Carmen
   Gina Cassill   Elaine Cassinis   Natalie L. Cato   Jennifer E. Caudle   Rogel Cayetano   Haluk Ceyhun   Mark Chacon
...Chavez   Paul Chelminiak   Hank C. Chen   Ling-Yi Chen   Nancy Chen   Kam Yee Cheng   Julie Chien   Dexter Chin
...n A. Clark   Kristine Clark   Robert Clark   Martha Clarkson   Kim Clement   Kathryn Prim   Brian Cloepfil   John Cochran
...llins   Julie Collins   Kim Collins   Lance A. Collins   Brian J. Collins-Friedrichs   Tracey L. Compton   Justin W. Cook
...land   Kimberly Corbin   Tom Cordelle   Tracy A. Corley   K.C. Correll   Tracy Corriveau   Todd W. Cota   Chuck Couey
   Michael Creighton   Garrett C. Cress   Cristine A. Cressler   Christian Crisologo   Lisa Crittenden   Margaret Cruse
   Curtis   Darryl J. Custer   Kelvin Dahlgren   Betsey Dailey   Peter J. Damento   Terri A. Daniel   Ditos B. Daranciang
...DeMille   Mackey Deasy   Lita deBoer   David Decker   Thomas Deering, Jr.   Laurel Defrang-Peterson   Anthony DeJesus
...evore   Carole Dewey   Jim Dewey   Clydell Dexter   Tonya Dickason   Drew Dickey   Malcolm Dickson   Dennis Dieni
   Kelly J. Dolan   Stefanie J. Dolman   Michael Doss   Kate Dougherty   Emily Dovey   Sandra D. Doyle   Cheryl Drake
...ing   Phu Duong   John Dwight   Kristi A. Dwight   Stephen Dwoskin   Kelly M. Earls   Jesus Eballar   Monica Echternkamp
...Eldemar   Stacy Eliot   Dak A. Elliott   Sarah C. Ellwood   Mark B. Elster   Diane L. Emick   Candace Eng   Terri Engberg
...Ereckson   Steven Erickson   Terri Lee Erickson   Laura Esther   Jacqui Evanchik   Jennifer Evangelist   Darci Evidon
...s   Janet Faulkner   Lana Faulkner   Cynthia S. Faw   Justin Fay   Beth Ferguson   R. Dennis Ferguson   Lora Fernandes
...Fleming   Robin Fleming   Collette Flink   Jana Flinn   Jennifer E. Floyd   C. Anthony Fodden   Esther Y. Foerderer
...hen P. Fox   Alex Fradkin   Susan J. Freeman   Chris Frost   Ken Fuller   Tracy Funderburk   Kate Furlong   Alan T. Furushima
...Galvez   Daniel Ganfield   Abraham Garcia, Jr.   Arthur E. Garcia   LeeAnn A. Garcia   Julie Gardner   Mitchell Gardner
...rron   Nichole Gerron   Oscar Gestoso   Elizabeth A. Ghaly   Mary-Jo Giamberardini   Greta M. Gillisse   Viviana Gilroy
...eson   Kimberly A. Golka   Wilfredo Gonzalez   James Goodboy   Phillip Goodman   Charles Gordon   Jody Gough
...aham   Kara Grahn   Tamara E. Gramer   Terry Granillo   Daniel Grant   Duane Grant   Jeremy R. Grant   Julie Grant
...Griffin   Ann Griffith   Marj Griggs   Kimberleigh D. Grimm   Elik Grin   Kersten Gronlund   April Gross   Douglas Grove
...Patricia Hahler   Laurel Haigh-Gore   Vivian Haight   Christopher J. Haine   Michelle M. Hajder   Arne Hall   Richard B. Hall
...ulie Hammerquist   Alta Hamoui   S. Denea Hanes   David E. Hansen   Eric Hanson   Bin Hao   Douglas Hardenburgh
...Haselow   Pamela Hatfield   Anja Haubold   Diana L. Hawkins   David Haynes   Jeffrey D. Haywood   Marguerite Thomas
...assandra A. Henderson   Gary Henderson   Michelle M. Henderson   Erin Hendricks   Michael Herman   Thomas F. Herrera
...aci Hiller   Annette Hillesland   Nick J. Hines   Paul A. Hjorten   LeeAnn Hobble   Robert Hobble   John W. Hoffman
...g   Stacey L. Hooper   Robert Hopkins   Sarah Hopkins   Ann Hopping   David Hornberg   Robert D. Horton   Tim Hossner
...vid Hudacek   Doug Huffman   Curtis Hughes   Jeffrey Hummel   Randall Hummer   Rebecca Humphries   Laurene Hungle
...Robert J. Hutnik   Romi K. Iassudo   Kim Inabnit   Crystal Inge   Diane Inouye   Joan Insel   Boris Iochev   Leigh R. Ishida
   Bruce James   David Jarrell   Lori J. Jay   Mischelle Jenkins   Nathan J. Jenkins   Kimberly A. Jennings   Jill Jensen
...rolyn Johnson   Gregg T. Johnson   Jayne L. Johnson   Lucy Johnson   Mark Johnson   Paul E. Johnson   Rodney Johnson
...ohnson-Newton   Heather Johnston   Carolyn G. Jones   Colleen R. Jones   Eric D. Jones   Lara Jones   Martin B. Jones
...namarie Kane   Steven Kane   Paul Kang   Ruth Kapcia   Amy Karol   William B. Karst   Roland Karsten   David R. Kase
...Clint Kendall   Judy Kennedy   Michelle Kenney   Richard D. Kenney   Joseph Kenny   John Kent-Russell   Diane Keppel
   Hah Chin Kim   Michelle J. Kim   Sung Min Kim   Tina S. Kim   Clement C. King   Richard King   Edward M. Kinney
...Knebel   Shannon D. Knepper   Eric Knudtson   Susanmarie Koenigs   David Kofahl   Teresa Kohoutek   Klarice Kolbe
...harles Krimmert   Linda Krippaehne   Margaret Kritzberger   Karen L. Krueger   Kevin Kuan   Erika Kuchar   Rachel M. Kuhn
...iam P. Lacey   Stanley T. Laegreid   Eric S. Lagerberg   Daniel Lai   Louise S. Lakier   Adrian Lam   Matthew Lamont
...gari   Hope Law   Stefanie L. Lawrence   Sheila Lawson   Elizabeth LeDorze   Elizabeth Leder   Celia Lee   Michael C. Lee
...D L. Lemmon   Jennifer Lenaghan   Kelly R. Leonard   Maureen Leonard   David Letrondo   Arnold Levin   Scott M. Lewis

# CALLISON

## CREATING SMARTER PLACES

CALLISON

ARCHIT

Visual Reference Publications, Inc.
302 Fifth Avenue
New York, NY 10001

Distributors to the trade in the United States and Canada:
Watson-Guptill
770 Broadway
New York, NY 10003

Distributors outside the United States and Canada:
HarperCollins International
10 East 53rd Street
New York, NY 10022-5299

Library of Congress Cataloging in Publication Data:
Callison: Creating Smarter Places
Printed in China
ISBN: 1-58471-043-8

front cover: **Ayala Center Greenbelt**
front flap: **Grand Gateway, FlatIron Crossing**
back cover: **Suwon Gateway Plaza, City Centre**
back flap: **Skymart at Chek Lap Kok**
All photographs by Chris Eden

Printed and bound in Hong Kong
Design and type composition by group c inc/New Haven (BC, JW, SC)

ECTURE

# CALLISON

## CREATING SMARTER PLACES

Text by Richard Rapaport
Edited by Brad Collins

Visual Reference Publications Inc., New York

CALLISON

CALLISON

# FOREWORD

### Getting to the Smarter Place

Over the past thirty years, Callison has emerged as a global leader in mixed-use and retail destinations by creating architecture that is a magnet for excitement and people at the same time that it is profitable and operationally sustainable — what we call a "smarter place."

We achieved this by accumulating substantial knowledge and insights from practicing in diverse cultures and across many different markets — filling our designers' toolbox with knowledge and insight that we access in all of our work, for all of our clients.

These smarter places have distinctive characteristics. They are destinations infused with character intrinsic to local culture and driven by the demands of the international marketplace. They are places that demonstrate how a client's business goals are best achieved when design focuses on the end user's aspirations and needs. It is using smarter practices to create simplicity out of complex problems. Smarter places occur when the depth of our specialist market expertise gives birth to a new creation, representing the highest form of market convergence as it sets a new industry benchmark.

By helping client after client successfully communicate and connect with audiences, we've seen our vision of smarter places become vital components of communities throughout the world. From Seattle to Shanghai, from Denver to Dubai, demand for world-class destinations is greater than ever, creating new opportunities to explore uncharted territory. With our project teams located around the world and by creating global alliances and collaborations that cross industry lines, Callison is now imagining the what, the how, the where, and the who of the next generation of smarter places.

# LIVING LOCALLY COMPETING GLOBALLY

Callison is one of the world's largest, most global design firms with more than four hundred employees and projects in North and South America, Europe, the Middle East and throughout Asia. Callison is also one of the world's largest, most local design firms, occupying five floors of City Centre in downtown Seattle.

From the beginning, Callison was deeply involved in the life, development and redevelopment of Greater Seattle and the Pacific Northwest region. As important as the projects it was creating, were the deep and — particularly for the one-hit-and-you're-out design industry — long-term relationships it was developing with the region's definitive companies. These included Nordstrom, Microsoft, Boeing, Nike, Eddie Bauer, Washington Mutual, Starbucks, Amazon.com and others, some of which drove Seattle's and the Northwest's most powerful surge to international prominence.

As designer to the corporate stars, some of that energy naturally rubbed off onto Callison especially during the early 1980s, when it was making the jump from local hero to international icon.

Fueling that energy was a three-pronged strategy that allowed Callison to export best-quality service around the world: custom-tailoring delivery systems in the client's best interests; a state-of-the-art approach to using technology and supporting a 24-hour global work schedule; and collaboration.

**BANK OF CHINA**
LOCATED IN THE GROWING PUDONG DEVELOPMENT AREA OF SHANGHAI, THE 32-STORY BANK OF CHINA TOWER PRESENTS A DRAMATIC IMAGE ON THE SHANGHAI SKYLINE.

As Callison began to extend its reach beyond the Northwest, the firm made a decision that makes it unique among the world's leading design firms. Rather than send partners off to set up offices in cities around the world — a typical way to grow — Callison decided to keep its team of experts together in Seattle, distributing expert teams as the project demands. This rational strategy places the creative value and knowledge directly on the project rather than on building or maintaining redundant administrative offices.

As part of the collaboration strategy, Callison formed Insight Alliance, a strategic alliance with design industry leaders that provides a multiple-office delivery platform through its allied partners' network of offices. And, since Callison is not focused on building a number of administrative offices, it does not have a competitive attitude toward local firms. This allows the firm to invest in partnerships to increase local insight, improve communications with entitlement agencies, share knowledge and increase effectiveness.

Callison believes it can live locally while it competes globally. Perhaps, "thrive locally" is a more accurate phrase.

**SPACE NEEDLE**
THE ADDITION OF A BASE PAVILION TO THE LANDMARK SPACE NEEDLE UPGRADES THE GUEST EXPERIENCE AND ENHANCES THE NEEDLE'S STATUS AS A SEATTLE ICON. RESEMBLING A TRANSPARENT NAUTILUS SURROUNDING THE THREE-LEGGED BASE OF THE SPACE NEEDLE, THE STRUCTURE IMPROVES QUEUING AND PROVIDES NEW RETAIL OPPORTUNITIES.

**DFS GALLERIA**
ONE OF 12 FLAGSHIP STORES FOR THE LUXURY BRAND EMPORIUM, DFS GALLERIA SINGAPORE IS DESIGNED TO REFLECT THE CITY'S DISTINCT HISTORY AND CULTURAL DIVERSITIES.

### Finding the Local Angle

Callison's zeal for getting at the details that matter to the customers, the employees, the guests or the patients — and anyone else who will use and experience their client's project — begins to explain the firm's attention to the specifics of locale. To Callison, finding a local angle is no more — and no less — than a design, business and market strategy rolled into one. So far, the strategy seems to have worked.

As the firm has helped transform Seattle into one of the most desirable and livable cities in the world, it has learned the value of tapping into the demographic, geographic, cultural and social specifics of a location. It has learned the value of transforming those specifics into a brand. And it has learned the importance of the relationships that people form with the places where they live and the places that they visit.

### Worldwide, Locally

Though Callison has chosen to centralize much of its creative talent in Seattle, it no longer lives only in Seattle. It now lives locally worldwide. Callison designers apply lessons learned over twenty-five years of working locally in Manila and Moscow, Shanghai and Dubai. Or Denver, Colorado, for that matter. Wherever it has its project, the firm deploys their people to become as familiar with a new locale as they are with Seattle.

**OLAYA PLACE**
LOCATED IN DOWNTOWN RIYADH, OLAYA PLACE IS DESIGNED TO ATTRACT BOUTIQUE RETAILERS AND RESTAURANTS, AS WELL AS CLASS A OFFICE TENANTS. THE OFFICE BUILDING EMPLOYS A VARIETY OF STRATEGIES TO ACHIEVE ENERGY EFFICIENCY, WHILE OFFERING GENEROUS FLOOR AREAS, HIGH CEILINGS AND FLEXIBLE OFFICE SPACE.

When they come back to the Callison "hothouse," projects simply take shape more quickly and surely. That's one of the advantages to the firm's approach. Another is that Callison has won more than its share of work in overseas markets. To date, the firm has designed projects in more than 20 countries

There are other pluses to being a diversified, global practice working together in a high-rise that the firm designed. Perhaps the most important of these is the ability to look out the window over a city that Callison has played no small part in shaping, and that works about as well as any city or region on the planet. This means that the solutions Callison is able to provide leave clients with the comfortable feeling that the solution for their project stands a pretty good chance of working in their locale as well.

**NORDSTROM SEATTLE**
CALLISON'S THREE-DECADE PARTNERSHIP WITH NORDSTROM INCLUDES THE RENOVATION OF A HISTORIC DEPARTMENT STORE BUILDING INTO THEIR NEW FLAGSHIP IN THE HEART OF DOWN-TOWN SEATTLE.

**MICROSOFT WORLD HEADQUARTERS**
CALLISON HAS BEEN WORKING WITH MICROSOFT SINCE 1985 TO DEVELOP THEIR WORLD HEADQUARTERS, PLANNING AND DESIGNING ITS COLLEGIATE-STYLE CAMPUS.

AYAL

AYALA CENTER GREENBELT

MANILA, PHILIPPINES

With an indigenous design that respects Manila's revered Greenbelt Park, Ayala Center Greenbelt has won praise for restoring and enhancing the natural environment, attracting major retailers from competing projects and establishing a true heart for the city.

### A Wide Mix of Uses, a Wide Variety of Duties

Manila is the heart of the Philippines, the Makati Central Business District (CBD) is the heart of Manila and the 38-hectare Ayala Center is the heart of Manila's CBD. In 2000, Ayala Land, Inc., developers of prestigious shopping and entertainment centers throughout Southeast Asia, awarded Callison the contract to create a master plan for the Greenbelt and environs. This shopping and entertainment complex is phase three of a multi-phased, multi-use destination.

### The Central Park of the Philippines

Ayala is not only one of the Philippines' oldest and largest landholders and developers, but it controls virtually all of the Makati CBD. For Ayala and Manilans in general, Greenbelt Park is a prized location, something like Central Park is to New Yorkers. The goal, therefore, needed to be a highly sensitive design solution that could complement and enhance the beloved Greenbelt Park.

Callison's master plan for Greenbelt uses a circulation system with raised pedestrian walkways and outdoor plazas to weave together the different components within the Center and the commercial district surrounding the park into a coherent neighborhood experience that, for the first time, creates a unified center to the heart of Manila.

## A Garden Wall

The new 300,000-square-foot Ayala Center Greenbelt is key to the master plan, carefully crafting a "garden wall" on the park side and meeting the lively, crowded streetscape on the other with a harder-edged and more commercial face.

On the park side of the "garden wall," a peaceful connection was made to the Park through a series of walkways, meandering landscaped courtyards and pathways, outdoor restaurants, cafés and plazas that brought the tropical forest of the park into the project.

## Indigenous Forms/Tropical Materials

The project itself was unlike any development Filipinos had seen in their lifetimes. Instead of being one of the blank-faced, internally focused, air-conditioned malls erected throughout the Philippines, the Callison design harkens back to the indigenous forms and tropical materials that are unique to Manila and its home island of Luzon.

Callison's design for Ayala Center Greenbelt includes three four-story pavilions crafted with an open-air design that links to an elevated covered walkway that is part of the master plan's conceived network of pedestrian thoroughfares. This network weaves together the entire complex and commercial district into an urban destination that residents, office workers and visitors can freely access and enjoy.

## A Surprising Mix of Uses

The Greenbelt plan includes two L-Shaped buildings with a grand plaza sweeping out from the buildings' convergence and stepping down into a garden below. Anchoring the project's north end, is the new, highly anticipated Ayala Museum. A courtyard outside the museum integrates both a chapel and a sculpture garden, while another courtyard incorporates an outdoor stage.

In addition to its roles as architect and master planner, Callison helped Ayala bring together a distinctive tenant roster. Ayala Center Greenbelt offers a mix of retail that goes far beyond the typically prosaic and similar lineup of stores. Many of the shops in the complex are local stores offering one-of-a-kind lines of merchandise and services.

## Escalating Modalities

Beginning with the museum at the north end of the project, Callison planned a very careful escalation of retail, restaurant and entertainment uses. Each pavilion houses progressively more extroverted tenants, beginning with the museum at the north end with "quiet" tenants like a bookstore and galleries, then rounding the intersection of Makati Avenue and Esperanza Street with home and fashion-oriented tenants and terrace restuarants, before finally turning west into a lively zone of music and video stores, dining, cinemas and nightclubs.

Since its opening in 2001, the Greenbelt developments have proven to be one of Asia's most notable success stories and have helped move Ayala into the elite of South Asian development. Drawing an average of 45,000 visitors a day, the project has become one of Manila's most talked about destinations—a sparkling setting from which to experience the jewel that is Greenbelt Park.

CITY CENTRE

SEATTLE, WASHINGTON

Built in 1988, City Centre remains Seattle's premier office address because it is so much more than an office building; its identity and vitality are the result of a diversity of experiences.

Occupying the block between Fifth and Sixth Avenues, and Union and Pike Streets, City Centre essentially shifted the center of Seattle's central business district. With its mix of uses, extended hours, inviting lobby spaces, innovative highrise design and unique collection of local and international retailers, the 44-story tower has remained downtown Seattle's most desirable office address for more than 15 years.

Home to U.S. Bank, three of Seattle's major law firms and Callison, the City Centre was the firm's first vertical mixed-use destination with a retail base supporting 41 office floors. With its angled walls that afford eighteen corner offices per floor, the building offers one of Seattle's most desirable highrise floorplates.

The three-story retail podium is anchored by Barney's of New York and Palomino, one of downtown Seattle's hottest hangouts and restaurants, a day care center and FAO Schwartz toy store. It may also be the only building in the world with three Starbucks Coffee locations.

City Centre was designed to do what all business district highrises aspire to but few achieve; to break out of the nine-to-five business day and to stay full, and making money, late into the night. On most nights, the building is full of downtowners and others who have decided to make an evening of it.

C E N T

## A Definitive Collection

The 150,000-square-foot atrium is also as inviting and comfortable as a private club, and beckons passersby to stop and sit in one of the comfortable chairs situated around the lobby. Once stopped, however, they tend to stay drawn to the glowing mahogany and glass cases holding what one critic described as "a stunning survey" of international glass by masters like Chihuly, William Morris and nearly 40 more artists of the Pilchuck Glass School. "The more one spends time at City Centre," this same writer noted, "the deeper one's appreciation of glass will be."

City Centre was designed
to do what many business
district highrises aspire
to but few achieve;
to break out of the
nine-to-five business day

# NORD
## NORDSTROM

MULTIPLE LOCATIONS, UNITED STATES

When it comes to client service, Callison has often been called the Nordstrom of designers; in its nearly 30-year collaboration, the firm has played an instrumental role in one of the great retail success stories in recent times.

### Volume and Depth

Since 1975, Callison has designed an extraordinary 17 million square feet of space for Nordstrom, including the last 124 Nordstrom stores in 24 American states, along with offices and data and distribution centers. Volume alone, however, does not adequately tell the story of a profound and deeply collaborative relationship between Nordstrom and Callison that has helped the store increase sales, enhance productivity, and realize a high return on investment. Callison provides Nordstrom with a virtual continuum of design services including site evaluation, retail planning, architecture, interior design, fixture design and construction administration services.

Simply put, Callison has played an instrumental role in one of the great retail success stories in recent times.

The reverse is also true. One of the hallmarks of Nordstrom's success is the way the store has redefined the meaning of customer service. Over the nearly three-decade collaboration, Nordstrom has provided Callison with an exemplar of all-consuming focus on the customer that has become a Callison hallmark.

And as Nordstrom has expanded into American cities and suburban shopping centers, Callison has aided in that growth by developing a specialty in shopping center design that has led to the creation of some of the most acclaimed and profitable destination retail in the world. Over the years, in working with Nordstrom, Callison has become so deeply involved in the business of shops, stores, malls and regional shopping centers, that the firm is now, independent of design and architecture, one of the leading retail consultants in the world.

STROM

## The Drive to Innovate

Since 1975, Callison has been helping Nordstrom improve on its legendary relationship with customers by developing innovative design concepts, many of which have become standard operating procedure in the retail industry. These include such now-standard practices as open floor plans to help customers navigate their way through often-unfamiliar storescapes; the introduction of family restrooms, an in-store must to lower the stress of parents with young children; and, the "open-sell" concept, which makes merchandise more accessible to time-pressured shoppers — a concept that made its debut in Nordstrom's cosmetics department. At the other end of the retail spectrum, "shop-til-you-droppers" feel unhurried and welcome as they try fashions on in the spacious, comfortable and private dressing rooms that are standard in every Nordstrom store.

As Nordstrom advanced to new levels of retailing, Callison's goal was to create a platform for extraordinary presentation and service that remained open to the inevitability of change. The mission from the start was to support Nordstrom's business goals with an infrastructure that would remain viable through evolving technology, fluctuating market opportunities and changing consumer tastes. That mission continues today.

COLLECTORS

As Nordstrom expanded across America in the last two decades, Nordstrom and Callison have maintained a quality and originality that, without exception, makes walking into a Nordstrom anywhere in the United States a singular experience with a design that leaves no question about the name inscribed outside.

# CREATING SMARTER PLACES
## Making Intelligent Choices in Mixed-Use Developments

**Callison has breathed life into some of the category's most definitive projects and won a reputation for bringing unprecedented design intelligence to mixed-use projects. Success, whether measured in terms of popular excitement, profitability per square foot or community acceptance, emphasizes Callison's position as the leading practitioner in the highly demanding discipline of mixed-use design.**

Mixed-use has many faces. It can be as straightforward as opening a Starbucks Coffee in the lobby of a Wells Fargo Bank. It can be as many-sided as building from scratch a new neighborhood on the outskirts of Kuala Lumpur. Mixed-use can look like an office complex that integrates stores, shops and restaurants to keep the lights on, the people strolling and the registers ringing beyond the nine-to-five working life of traditional downtown offices.

Mixed-use can be an office/residential highrise project built on an underutilized property next to a busy rail station. Enhancing both revenue and renown, it can be a multi-story enclosed shopping center with a vibrant restaurant/entertainment district.

Callison has designed each of these projects as well as a number of other successful mixed-use types. So different are one from another that it would seem impossible at first look to characterize them as a single design category. But in Callison's world, they are.

### Making it Smart

Neither size nor particular usages are defining issues in mixed-use. Rather, it is the capacity of a project to accommodate more than one of the various needs of target users. Modern life is a complex ballet of multiple uses; people work, they commute, they eat, they relax, sleep, shop, learn, entertain, dream and so on. So if people are smart enough to lead multiple lives, then should not the places in which they live, work, play and shop also be smart enough to support the multiple uses?

"Mixed-use" could as easily be called "intelligent design for the modern condition." Even more to the point, mixed-use could and probably should be identified with the ideal toward which all facets of Callison design aims and to which its motto points: "Creating Smarter Places."

For Callison, the attributes that define a "smart place" are also key predicates of successful mixed-use. Although smart places are not always mixed-use, at least not yet, successful mixed-use places need to be designed with the built-in intelligence characteristic of a smart place.

The starting point of a high-IQ design begins with an important realization on the part of owners: that corporate real estate can be as important and potentially valuable for success as a base of seasoned employees or a fat portfolio of patents. Smart design can take real estate and make it a hardworking contributor to a company's creativity and profitability.

In this respect, "smart places" have a good deal in common with "smart employees," both potentially the kinds of corporate stars whose efforts contribute so heavily to the ultimate success of a company.

They work long hours. Development is too risky and expensive these days not to expect real estate to be working and creating value beyond traditional business hours. Hotels have long recognized that a ground floor restaurant/bar busy until all hours is not only a potential moneymaker, but can also help to keep the buzz going and beds filled.

**1700 SEVENTH**
WITH TIMELESS ARCHITECTURE THAT PROVIDES MODERN CLASS A OFFICE AND RETAIL SPACE, 1700 SEVENTH AVENUE IS DESIGNED TO FIT A MAJOR TENANT'S NEEDS, AND PROVIDE FLEXIBLE MULTI-TENANT SPACE, WHILE ANCHORING RETAIL GROWTH IN AN EMERGING DOWNTOWN NEIGHBORHOOD.

**SUWON GATEWAY PLAZA**
A LANDMARK REGIONAL MIXED-USE CENTER FOR THE CITY OF SUWON, A HISTORIC CITY NEAR SEOUL, KOREA, SUWON GATEWAY PLAZA IS CONCEIVED AS THE "CIVIC LIVING ROOM" FOR THE DIVERSE LIFESTYLES THAT MAKE UP ITS URBAN SURROUNDINGS.

They make money for the business. Today, developers do not have the luxury of time to incrementally balance a project's different uses and the component parts of a single use. There is a Darwinian imperative that measures success in terms of weeks and months rather than years. The mix of uses and other issues needs to be considered by experts, who understand how important it is to begin to turn profits without a long shakedown cruise.

They are flexible: To take advantage of emerging trends or new business opportunities, a project design must have built-in flexibility, both in terms of project phasing and for future use. Being able to shift gears with speed and decisiveness can be the difference between success and failure.

They have a life of their own: Economic self-sufficiency in today's tough economy is both difficult and essential. To get off the economic ventilator requires nothing less than the transformation of a project from an unknown quantity into a living, breathing part of its community. This is no small thing and requires that connections be developed on many different levels. Design can help what is ultimately a mutual seduction by providing visual clues to the themes in common that will create the bond between designed space and the user of that space. If the tryst is successful, the project will become an organic presence in its community.

**WELLS FARGO/STARBUCKS**
IN AN INNOVATIVE CONCEPT THAT MAKES THE MOST OF EXCESS BANK REAL ESTATE, WELLS FARGO AND STARBUCKS TEAMED UP TO OFFER BANKING, COFFEE AND OTHER DAILY SERVICES. TENANTS BENEFIT FROM A PRIME LOCATION AND CROSS-SELLING OPPORTUNITIES, WHILE CONSUMERS GET A ONE-STOP ERRAND AND MEETING PLACE WITH LONGER HOURS.

However, as Dr. Frankenstein and hundreds of developers have discovered over the years, creating a living organism, whether human or social, may be a simple concept to grasp, but is a difficult accomplishment to pull off.

**CARILLON POINT**
CARILLON POINT IS A VIBRANT SHORESIDE COMMUNITY WITH AN EXCEPTIONAL BLEND OF SERVICES, AMENITIES AND ACTIVITIES THAT TAKE FULL ADVANTAGE OF ITS 31-ACRE SITE ALONG LAKE WASHINGTON. AN ACTIVE CENTRAL PLAZA IS RINGED BY OFFICE, RETAIL, RESTAURANT AND HOTEL FACILITIES, WHICH ARE ORIENTED TO MAXIMIZE VIEWS OF THE LAKE.

### Creating Destinations

When a mixed-use project is successful at transcending its "job description" and becomes an organic and embraced part of its community, it can then be called by a name that is the highest mixed-use accolade: a destination.

In the mixed-use world according to Callison, a destination can be a shopping center, an office building or resort hotel, but it must be a place where people feel good, where they like to visit for no particular reason except that it feels right.

Creating a mixed-use destination is a smart long-term business strategy and one that virtually no other design firm can pull all the different components together so well. The ability to leverage diverse commercial categories in a single location creates a gravitational pull that far surpasses the draw of individual components. This in turn creates the buzz that tells people this is a special place, one that needs to be "checked out." In other words, a destination.

### Managing Complexity

Given the uniqueness of each assignment, Callison begins virtually anew each time a mixed-use project is addressed. The variables involved in successful mixed-use are staggering in number and complexity.

Successful mixed-use requires, for example, that the mix of use types, design character and underlying business objectives be tailored to location, site condition, political and permitting constraints, end-user profiles, market conditions and other variables.

Another level of complexity is added by the need to determine, on a very fine-tuned level, what the specific mix of uses is going to be. Not all uses are totally compatible. A residential component needs privacy, for example, while the retail portion demands visibility.

The prospect of mixed-ownership is equally confounding, necessitating that issues such as shared property lines, service access, and HVAC redundancies be hammered out in design. Callison understands these intricacies and has the tools to craft a balanced solution.

This is particularly good news for executives running development companies who stake their careers on the outcome of major projects. Good news as well that Callison's mixed-use methodology, like those in its other areas of practice, has a definite business bias; Callison owns one of the most enviable records in business design because it places tremendous credence on helping its clients reach their strategic goals and increase their profitability by designing places that pay their own way.

KUSI
THE FUTURE HOME OF KUSI-TV, OFFICES, HOTEL AND RESIDENTIAL, OCCUPIES A PROMINENT SITE IN SAN DIEGO'S MARINA DISTRICT. CALLISON VACATED A PORTION OF A CITY STREET TO CREATE A MAJOR PUBLIC PLAZA AND STRENGTHEN THE CONNECTION BETWEEN THE NEARBY CHILDREN'S PARK, TROLLEY STOP, AND CONVENTION CENTER. THE DESIGN DRAWS INSPIRATION FROM THE REGION'S HISTORIC SPANISH COLONIAL STYLE, ADAPTED TO A HIGHRISE STRUCTURE.

### Connecting with the Community

Callison begins the design process by "getting under the skin" of its clients. Learning to think and act like a client means that Callison is able to design spaces that align precisely with their business strategies. Similarly, Callison delves deeply into the physical, intellectual and emotional lives of the project's desired end users. Knowing the target audience in a profound way enables Callison to design toward emotional and intellectual archetypes that are in turn capable of getting under the skin of the people by whom the project is ultimately judged: the users.

Sometimes the archetypes tapped into are geographical, sometimes demographic or social. In all cases, they strive to find the most powerful connective tissue between a project and its users. Callison excels in this process of creating a brand that people will come to know and love.

### Connecting with the Team

To bring a mixed-use project to life certainly requires great design. Great design, however, is not enough for mixed-use.

A project team that can actually pull off the mixed-use balancing act needs to be choreographed in order to achieve the massive collaboration, coordination and communication effort required by the complicated design, phasing and construction stages of these projects.

Callison's skill in this area, the ability to facilitate and balance, to bring clarity and purpose to a diverse project workforce is at least as critical as design itself. With its organizational and communication skills, Callison can galvanize project teams in a way that, as in mixed-use itself, the sum becomes greater than the parts.

**MEYDENBAUER**
RE-CASTING MEYDENBAUER'S SUPERBLOCK MIXED-USE DEVELOPMENT INTO A BOLD CIVIC VISION PLAYED A KEY ROLE IN PUSHING THE PROJECT FORWARD.

### Leveraging the Experience

How did Callison get so good at mixed-use? Key is the firm's understanding of and focus on the business requirements of the client, as well as an in-house mastery of all of the many design, code and entitlement elements of each piece of the project, and an ability to develop the mix of uses at a precise enough level to approximate successful "organic" communities.

Another, non-design related factor is the firm's powerful network of relationships that enable it to bring the right players together to create a smart business fit. Callison is often at the table from the very start of a project. When, for example, a hotel operator for a development needs to be chosen or a funding plan created, the firm is there with expertise in areas few design firms can match.

In the final analysis, Callison recognizes that in mixed-use, the tiniest advantage can make a critical difference. Thus, the firm does not believe that there is such as thing as a minor element. The ability to create the necessary synergy between elements of a project is a calculation that has less to do with the size or importance of that element, than its ability to work with the others in catalyzing brand recognition and success.

### Not an End in Itself

Doing mixed-use simply to do mixed-use is to misunderstand the singular quality and calibrated thinking that goes into each project. For Callison, mixed-use is and will remain a vital tool with which to create viable communities and a lens through which design can be viewed in new and profoundly useful ways.

**SAN FRANCISCO GIANTS HEADQUARTERS**
THE GIANTS BUILDING AT PACIFIC BELL PARK FEATURES RETAIL, ENTERTAINMENT AND DINING ALONG SAN FRANCISCO'S WATERFRONT, HELPING TO TURN THE GIANTS HOME INTO A YEAR-ROUND ENTERTAINMENT DESTINATION.

GRA

GRAND GATEWAY

SHANGHAI, CHINA

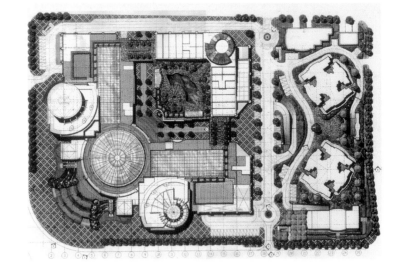

The largest mixed-use project attempted up to that time in China, Shanghai's Grand Gateway was also the most commercially successful development in the city's first generation of new buildings, thanks to painstaking integration, keen retail thinking and flexible design that hedged against the volatile property market.

### A Unique Skill Set

When Callison began design in 1993, the Grand Gateway complex was the largest project under development in the rapidly modernizing city of Shanghai as well as the most integrated mixed-use project underway. Grand Gateway combines twin 52-story towers with office and luxury residential uses that rise over 1.1 million square feet of retail and entertainment, flanked by one block of 9-story and one block of 11-story service apartments, and across Grand Avenue, two additional 34-story high-end residential towers.

Shanghai took to Grand Gateway immediately. Occupying a premium site at the Xu Jia Hui subway station, Grand Gateway would tap into the stream of over 250,000 commuters who passed through Shanghai's busiest transit hub daily.

A successful outcome was not nearly as apparent in late 1993, a time when 20 percent of the construction cranes in the world were in Shanghai and over 30 million square feet of commercial space was under development. After 8 months of unsuccessful attempts to obtain administrative approvals for the masterplan, Hong Kong developers Hang Lung Development Co. and its partners, Henderson Land Development and Haysan Development Co., hired Callison to take over the project — the developers' first venture into the burgeoning, but volatile mainland China construction market.

With significant investment dollars burning at an unacceptable rate, Callison re-launched the planning process with a more rational business approach, engaging the building and planning officials in the solution. From contracting with Callison on November 24 to masterplan approval on January 10, Grand Gateway made its way through Shanghai's labyrinthine process in less than two months, an unprecedented period. With approval came several important added dimensions to the project; Callison was also able to negotiate greater flexibility and a more viable plan.

N D G A

For example, fire safety had become a critical issue. A number of expensive or impractical solutions had been proposed and rejected and the situation was at an impasse. Recognizing that Shanghai officials had no experience with the kind of design proposed, Callison suggested that a Shanghai planning official join the design team. To deal with the fire safety issues, Callison sponsored a trip to Seattle for Shanghai fire officials where they could see firsthand how similar projects handled the problem. Not only did this produce a rapid approval of the design, but it formed the foundation for the code that is today applied to all commercial buildings in Shanghai.

## Market Flexibility

Recognizing the volatility of the market and the overabundance of commercial space under development in Shanghai, Callison worked with Hang Lung to design flexibility into the project from the start. Setting in place a multi-phased strategy for the entire complex, each component was designed to be economically and operationally viable even if development of subsequent parts was delayed. And, in fact, when reality hit and new commercial space far outpaced demand, Grand Gateway was one of the few projects that remained on a steady build-out course and captured strong occupancy.

## Smart-Place Design

More attention was applied to the flexibility of the office tower design. One tower was designated by the government as the tallest building allowed in this section of Shanghai, with a height requirement to accommodate a Doppler radar weather station. To gain the desired space and efficiency, Callison negotiated with the city to allow two towers of equal height, subsequently creating the symbolic "gateway" symmetry that is a desirable quality in the *feng shui* design aesthetic.

At the same time, the two towers incorporated a flexibility that would ensure the project against any of the often-severe market shifts endemic to the Chinese development market. Both towers are designed in such a way that the cores allowed either office use, or, if market conditions dictated, high-end residential.

Callison "smart-place" design innovations are evident in the Grand Gateway's entry staircase, the project's front door. By taking the novel approach of raising the entrance to the shopping center to a second level of the building, the stairway becomes a monumental announcement of Grand Gateway's presence at the commercial district's major intersection. Not only does this give the mall two retail-enhancing ground floors, but also has the effect of capturing rush-hour foot traffic from the street and rail station.

As conceived by Callison, urban mixed-use extends heavy use beyond normal business hours. In this mode, Grand Gateway has become Shanghai's nighttime venue of choice, attracting thousands of shoppers to the finely tuned mix of stores, service outlets, restaurants and nightclubs that populate the project's retail center. The center has also become a favorite among local residents who have made Grand Gateway's themed entertainment districts and its Paris-styled shopping street a regular evening stop.

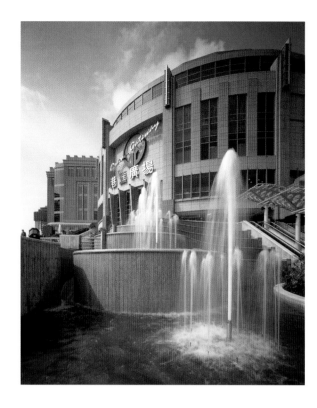

# SU

## SUWON GATEWAY PLAZA

SUWON, KOREA

Located above the Suwon Railway Station, Gateway Plaza capitalizes on the activity generated by the 30 million commuters who travel between Seoul and the perimeter city of Suwon each year with a vertical mixed-use design conceived as a "civic living room."

### A Mixed-Use Trend

Anchoring shopping and entertainment venues on or nearby major transportation hubs has become an increasingly common development model as urban centers grow more and more dense. The Suwon Gateway Plaza, a retail-driven mixed-use development, located on top of and around the main rail station in Suwon, South Korea, a high-tech center and university city southwest of Seoul, is just such a project.

Working with Aekyung Land Company, the development arm of Korea's premier department store chain, and the Suwon Transit Authority, Callison was commissioned to master plan and design the nearly 125,000-square-meter complex to capitalize on the activity generated by the more than 30 million commuters that pass through the station yearly.

WON

Key to the master plan was the need to establish a strong architectural identity that would enliven the everyday quality of commuting, while still providing clear access to and from the railway station. Integrating the needs of both the anchor retailer and the transit authority, Callison's solution was to make Suwon Plaza a "civic living room," an inviting and comfortable community center as well as a premier shopping and entertainment destination.

Suwon Gateway Plaza is the first and largest of its kind in Korea to offer the tenant mix, public spaces and amenities, such as office space, food court and entertainment center all in one location. The six-story center is divided into three distinct zones: the Lifestyle/Fashion zone, provided in the department store; the Gateway zone created by the railway station; and, the Adventure zone that includes the entertainment offerings of a multi-screen cinema, restaurants and cultural center.

Callison also designed the 230,000-square-foot Aekyung Department Store; Callison was brought on board to help the chain reach its goal of becoming one of the top department stores in Korea by 2010. To achieve this, the store's design focuses on two key criteria: to create a brand identity for Aekyung that stands out in the vendor-driven Korean market and to develop strong and resilient visual merchandising principles.

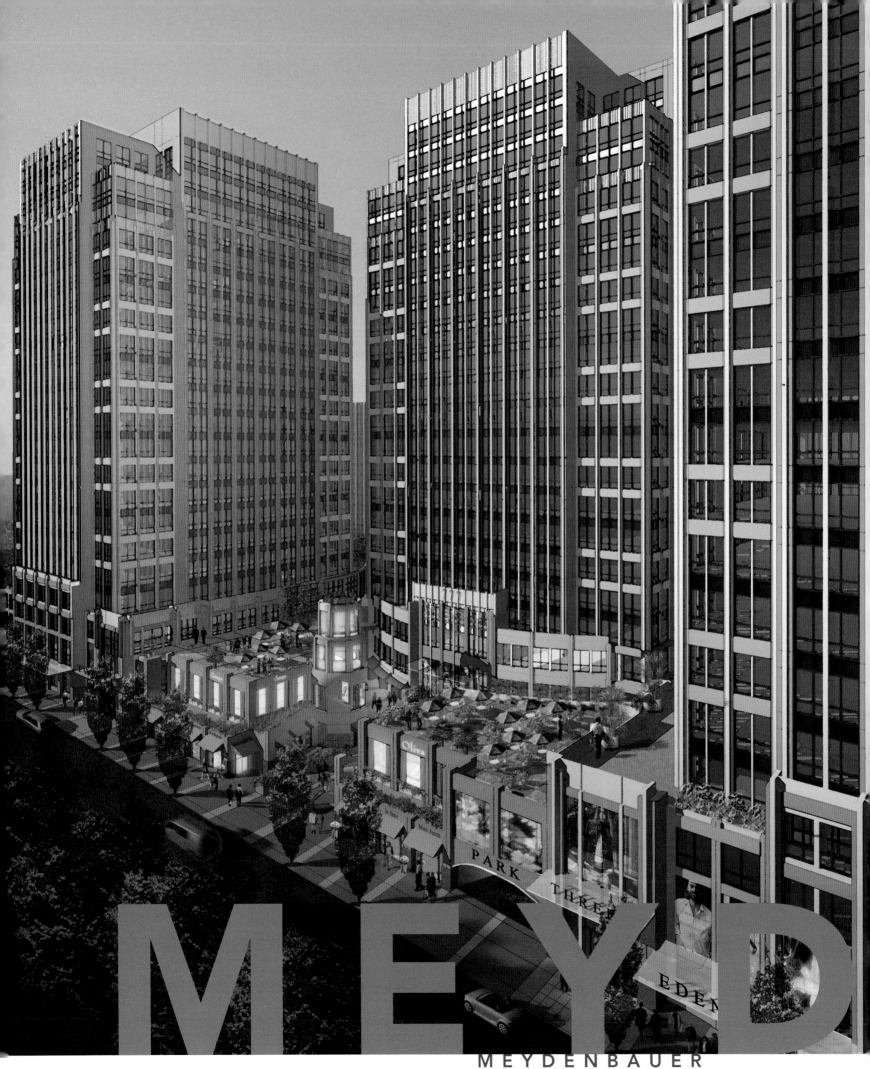

MEYD

MEYDENBAUER

BELLEVUE, WASHINGTON

**Recasting Meydenbauer's superblock mixed-use development into a bold civic vision played a key role in pushing the project forward.**

### Upping the Ante

In early 2003, developer Schnitzer Northwest LLC vastly upped the ante for the site adjacent to the Meydenbauer Civic Center in Bellevue across Lake Washington from Seattle. Instead of one hotel and a single office tower, the new plan presented a spectacular one-million-square-foot development including a 175-room executive residence hotel, a 450-room four-star hotel and three 400,000-square-foot office towers, as well as 175,000 square feet of retail at the base of the towers, plus a 3,500-car parking garage underneath the entire complex.

### Nothing Less than "Breathtaking"

The expanded vision showed tremendous confidence on the part of both Schnitzer and Callison. Two previous owners of the 217,000-square-foot parcel had been unable to get projects off the ground, the last of the two selling the parcel to Schnitzer in 2000. Based on their combined research, both developer and designer determined that the key to success was a vision that is nothing less than breathtaking. Anything less on this showcase site would risk failure.

Breathtaking the plans were: A tree-lined porte cochere sweeps up to the two adjacent hotels and office towers that step up the hill on the north side of the site. Shop-lined pedestrian promenades on several different levels wind around the office towers, creating a retail passage reminiscent of Europe's great shopping streets. On the street side, the retail edge is integrated with the office towers, presenting a grand urban facade.

### A Modular Strategy

Critical to the plan's acceptance was the modular and phased design that calls for the different components to be built in stages over the next seven years. The pace of development can respond to the speed of the economy and local market conditions and provide an opportunity for the community to "absorb" the development over time.

ENBAU

ACT

ACT THEATRE

SEATTLE, WASHINGTON

In doing its business, political, planning and artistic best to build a new home for ACT, the Pacific Northwest's premier contemporary theater company, Callison proved itself the master of each of those elements.

### Skilled at the Deal, Schooled in Design

Callison is as skilled in the art of the deal as it is schooled in the science of design. It took great amounts of both talents to transform a boarded-up landmark auditorium in downtown Seattle into one of the nation's most elegant and functional regional theater complexes.

Working within the complex world of public/private development and historic preservation, the firm leveraged ACT's nonprofit status, a landmark site, available low-income housing monies and other tax and grant incentives to build a home for the Pacific Northwest's most notable contemporary stage group.

### Out of One, Three

A project in which political, regulatory and funding concerns proved to be as challenging as the design itself, Callison was the moving force behind the transformation of downtown Seattle's historic-but-rundown Eagles Auditorium building. The result was a new space for ACT, accommodating two 360-seat performing arts spaces, a third, more flexible performance space, a workshop and administrative areas, along with a low-income housing component on the top levels.

THEA

## Vision

When Callison proposed renovating the 1925-vintage Eagles Auditorium, ACT didn't see how the building could be transformed into a workable space. At its most persuasive, Callison presented plans that finally did convince ACT executives that the requirements of their highly specific and demanding events program could be met.

As architect for the project, the team orchestrated the large number of often-conflicting interests, including the restoration of the exterior, accommodating the affordable housing (designed by another architect) and creating a pedestrian connection to parking at the Convention Center.

The architecture was also a complex challenge, requiring the adaptation of the building to create three very different theater experiences: one, the very technical theater-in-the-round vision of the artistic director; another a flexible, cabaret-style space and a third as a traditional "thrust" stage that projected beyond the proscenium to maintain the actor-audience intimacy for which ACT is known.

In the Arena theater, the size and arrangement of the extensive technical lighting and sound facilities required by ACT's vision made integration into the building unsuitable. Instead, suspending the equipment in the space touches the original fabric as lightly as possible, to preserve historic character and substance.

Premiering in 1996, the new building has proven to be a fitting home and an exciting venue for ACT. The benefits are many; returning a sadly unused building to public life, preserving a landmark and adding a key corner piece to downtown Seattle's revitalization jigsaw puzzle.

# ON
## ONE CONVENTION PLACE

SEATTLE, WASHINGTON

Despite complexities arising from air rights, a landmark neighbor and multiple stake-holders, both public and private, One Convention Place was fully leased the day it was completed.

### The Price of Success

One Convention Place is the centerpiece of a mixed-use development sparked by the decision to expand the Washington State Convention and Trade Center, a move that set off the revitalization of Seattle's urban core. It has been a successful addition to Seattle's downtown skyline — from the day it opened in late 2000, space in the sixteen-story, 308,000-square-foot office tower has been fully leased.

### Careful Configuration

Notoriously tricky, urban mixed-use is also vital to maximizing the property values and pumping life into today's downtown areas. Making it work in the case of One Convention Place required creativity, patience and persistence: The setting was unique and the design challenges thorny. One Convention Place was an air rights building sitting above the convention center's new entrance.

By giving the tower its own distinctive lobby entrance off Seventh Avenue, it also solved the problem of how to have a street presence for a building that essentially starts 120 feet above ground level.

### Worth the Effort

Despite all of the challenges, the results made the process worthwhile and created a truly unique structure with such acknowledged design innovations as its air rights placement, its shared street-level lobby and grand new entry with the convention center. Most important, the success of One Convention Place gave a financial boost to the project as a whole, contributing to the realization of the three-block addition to the convention center and the revitalization of Seattle's urban core.

E CON

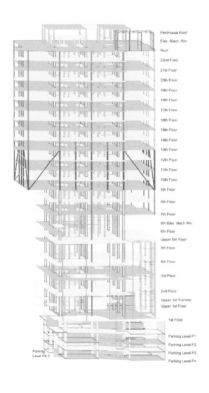

CARI

CARILLON POINT

KIRKLAND, WASHINGTON

Located on the shores of Lake Washington near Seattle, Carillon Point was one of the first waterfront mixed-use developments in the United States, and remains one of the most vibrant.

Constructed in multiple phases, and opened in 1989, Carillon Point was one of the first mixed-use waterfront developments in the United States and remains one of the most successful. Located on the eastern shore of Lake Washington, this 31-acre mixed-use development is home to major corporations, signature restaurants, luxurious yachts, waterfront condominiums, a hotel; as well as a destination for visitors from around the region and beyond.

The project has been tremendously successful from a business point of view and embraced as a community asset. Carillon Point consistently maintains the highest occupancy and highest per-square-foot lease rates in the region, and continues to feed off the energy and vitality generated by the office workers, hotel guests, shoppers, diners, boaters and pedestrians enjoying the waterfront, the water, and the mountain views.

Carillon Point is organized around a central plaza, one end of which is open to the water and the other enclosed by two of the site's buildings. Six carillons, the bell towers that give the project its name, chime on the hour. The carillons — situated around a platform designed for musical presentations, public events and other gatherings — provide an effective focal point for the plaza, as well as a strong identifying architectural element.

L L O N

CARILLON POINT

### Maximizing Lake Views

Retail, office and dining facilities are located around the perimeter of the plaza, creating effective synergy between the various elements of the project. Two grand staircases mask the structured parking and connect the plaza to the fishing pier and the public esplanade that parallels the waterfront. Positioned to maximize access to lake views, Carillon Point's offices and shops are also visible from Lake Washington Boulevard.

### An Immense Transformation

Carillon Point has undergone such a tremendous transformation that it is difficult to conceive of it as it was in the early 1980s, an abandoned shipyard on environmentally sensitive wetlands. As huge as the change has been, the equally gigantic hurdles faced by Callison may explain why Carillon Point remains the only project of its type in the Northwest. The planning process for Carillon Point remains a textbook case of how patient persuasion and making a true connection with the community can pay off.

As a gesture of goodwill to citizens of Kirkland, who had long battled to keep the Carillon Point Shipyards open and for the cleanup of one of the region's most toxic sites, even with the developer's offer to perform the cleanup with private funds, the project still required hundreds of neighborhood and town meetings, which Callison participated in and facilitated. Slowly, public opinion turned in favor of the project, with some of the most vehement critics becoming strong advocates.

### The Sum Total

Engaging the waterfront with public amenities, designing low-profile, brick buildings tiered up the sloping site to maintain views and blend with the residential character of surrounding condominiums and integrating nearly two thousand parking spaces below the corporate offices were all strategies that helped create a place that achieves not only the developer's vision, but also those of the community and the planning authority.

In the end, designers, public officials, residents of the community, workers and weekend visitors all agree that the agreement so carefully crafted and painstakingly worked out, has created a destination that is a source of pride for the region.

GARD

ANAHEIM GARDENWALK

ANAHEIM, CALIFORNIA

GardenWalk's shopping, dining and entertainment activities will form a key link between Anaheim's Resort District, Convention Center and Disneyland's California Adventure Theme Park.

### Complementing City Redevelopment

Envisioned as a complement to the redevelopment activities planned for downtown Anaheim, GardenWalk is the initial phase of a 29-acre mixed-use outdoor retail and entertainment center.

Developed by Price Legacy, Inc. of San Diego, the project will be built in phases; the first, GardenWalk, includes retail, restaurant and entertainment. The second phase — Garden District — scheduled for completion in 2010, will include the four on-site hotels providing more than 1,600 rooms and an aquarium.

### The Market Magic of Mixed-use

In a project of this scale, the ability to quickly adjust phasing in response to changing economic conditions is a tribute to its mixed-use composition and to the architects who are the design world's leading proselytizers for the benefits of mixed-use solutions. Without placing all the development "eggs" in a single-use "basket," important, and often project-sustaining flexibility, profitability and cost savings can be achieved.

### An Insightful Alliance

Flexibility and cost reduction were also key to another kind of innovation that was helping move GardenWalk to realization. Instead of the costly solution of a different architect for each mixed-use specialty, at GardenWalk that problem was solved by bringing on board Insight Alliance, a consortium of leading firms with the expertise as well as the experience working together on projects such as this. Callison, one of the founders of the Alliance, designed the retail, restaurant, entertainment and common areas of GardenWalk, while fellow Insight Alliance member Wimberly Allison Tong & Goo concentrated on the hotels.

EN WAL

SAN F

## SAN FRANCISCO GIANTS HEADQUARTERS

SAN FRANCISCO, CALIFORNIA

By creating a vital, urban destination that complements the adjoining stadium while generating a life of its own, the Giants Headquarters helps transform a seasonal business into a 365-day-a-year entertainment organization.

### A Transformation to 12X365

The San Francisco Giants are one of Major League Baseball's most venerable and forward-looking franchises. The Giants front-office envisioned a transformation from a seasonal business into a 365-day-a-year entertainment organization. In the midst of designing and constructing their new home, Pacific Bell Park, Giants CEO, Peter Magowan, recognized an opportunity to increase the value of the team by adding a vital, urban destination adjacent to the new stadium. Understanding that the stadium would be a new city icon, the question was posed, how to tap into this new asset beyond the 80 days of baseball. The Giants turned to Callison to explore some options.

### A Giants Gateway

Callison's solution was simple but creative, a structure that stays open year round, promoting the Giants and acting as a gateway into the stadium during the season. Retail outlets are located on the ground floor with franchise offices above.

In its final form, the project includes a three-story, mixed-use building housing 30,000 square feet of corporate office space for the Giants organization as well as the ground-level 5,000-square-foot San Francisco Giants new "Dugout" store and Willie Mays Restaurant drawing fans before and after the games.

# R A N C

Thanks to a cross-studio team of retail, workplace and graphic designers, the structure was seamlessly integrated into the stadium, while the retail and corporate headquarters were unified into a continuous branded environment.

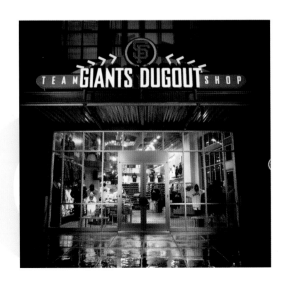

# HOSPITALITY AS AN ATTITUDE
## How Hospitality Strategies Enhance the User Experience

**It's one thing to create a hospitable experience at a resort, quite another to do so in a hospital, a store, an office or a shopping center. Or is it? No matter what the venue happens to be, the goal is always and simply to create an experience that makes people feel welcome, comfortable and special.**

Callison has impeccable credentials in hospitality design. In addition to playing a critical role in the creation of one of the last decade's only new hotel chains, the firm has completed successful hotel, resort and leisure residential developments all over the world. Ironically, Callison does not view hospitality as a design type so much as an attitude that can influence and enhance any project. It is an attitude that Callison applies to all design types, an attitude that recognizes the importance of creating a place — whether a store, a shopping center, a residential development or a hospital — where people feel welcome and comfortable.

For Callison, hospitality is a way of looking at, initiating and coloring an experience in a way that draws a person back to repeat that pleasurable experience. Hospitality plays on a number of different emotions and senses. It is part familiarity, part ease, part hopefulness, part groundedness, part sense of

**RAFFLES**
RAFFLES HOTEL IS A SINGAPORE LAND-
MARK WITH A RICH AND EXOTIC HISTORY.
THE MUSEUM STORE REFLECTS THE
TRADITIONAL ELEGANCE OF THE
ARCHITECTURE AND REINFORCES
THE HOTEL'S COLONIAL CHARACTER.

**BELLEVUE ATHLETIC CLUB**
AS AN AMENITY FOR ITS MEMBERS, THIS SOCIAL AND ATHLETIC CLUB ADDED A 70-ROOM HOTEL TO ITS FACILITIES. BY DEFINING A GRACIOUS COURTYARD ENTRANCE AND USING NATURAL MATERIALS IN SIMPLE, SCULPTED FORMS, THE NEW BUILDING'S DESIGN CREATES A MORE REFINED EXPERIENCE FOR MEMBERS AND THEIR GUESTS.

control, part being made to feel special. It is smart business to make customers and potential customers feel special and welcome. And it is a public service to design places that make people feel good when they go there.

Hospitality can be communicated in many different forms — a formal porte cochere staffed with valets at the entrance to a shopping center, an open floor plan at a department store enabling shoppers to see where they are and stay oriented, an overstuffed couch in the lobby of a hotel that makes it impossible not to sit down.

It can be created by including a series of small shops and galleries in a resort that enables a guest to browse and buy without having to drive into town. It can even be achieved by incorporating quality furniture and finishes in a hospital room that gives a patient the sense that comfort and individuality are as important as the convenience of the cleaning staff.

What these features have in common is their role in the creation of a "destination," the kind of place that people choose to return to, places they select over others.

### Familiarity

If hospitality is an attitude, then it is one created by the subtle evocation of different emotions and combinations of senses. For the Callison designer, it is almost like composing a musical score. The bass notes, the foundation upon which the score is set is the essence of familiarity. In design, "familiarity" does not, as the saying goes, "breed contempt," instead, something closer to "content" and "connectedness."

When Callison begins a project, it does so with some novel methods and goals. The firm incorporates disciplines not normally associated with their craft — demography, sociology, history, iconography and others. The designer is looking for archetypes, whether they are historical, geographic, mythical, regional, local or individual. The goal is to find the symbols that enable the design to connect with project users in a personal way.

**HARBOR STEPS**
PROJECT GOALS FOR HARBOR STEPS INCLUDED ESTABLISHING THE SITE AS A FOCAL POINT OF THE SURROUNDING AREA, PROVIDING LINKAGES FROM THE WATERFRONT FOR THE UPTOWN NEIGHBORHOODS, CREATING A SERIES OF PUBLIC SPACES AND ENSURING A STRONG WATER-TO-LAND PERSPECTIVE. PHASE I DESIGN OF THE RESIDENTIAL AND RETAIL COMPONENT COMPLEMENTS THE PUBLIC PLAZA AND ESTABLISHES THE DEVELOPMENT AS AN ATTRACTIVE URBAN NEIGHBORHOOD.

SCOTTSDALE FASHION SQUARE
THE EXPANSION OF SCOTTSDALE FASHION
SQUARE CONNECTS WITH THE COMMUNITY,
BOTH PHYSICALLY AND PSYCHOLOGICALLY. THE
CENTER IS ORIENTED TOWARD TOWN WITH NEW
RESTAURANTS AND OUTDOOR SEATING AND A
NEW RETAIL BRIDGE OVER A MAJOR ARTERIAL.
THE CENTER ALSO CELEBRATES THE STYLE OF
ARIZONA' S DESERT RESORTS WITH INVITING
LOBBIES AND A FORMAL PORTE COCHERE.

### Oriented

Good hosts do not let their guests get lost, and providing design reference points to help orient customers is both good manners and part of the hospitality palette. Once upon a time, it would be the practice of department stores to obscure sight lines so that customers would get lost on a floor and wander around various departments in an attempt to find their way out. The theory seems to have been that the more lost the customers got, the more they would end up buying.

Today, while there are stores that seem to prey on the aimlessly wandering, there is a new, hospitality-driven retail philosophy that believes an oriented customer is a happy shopper. This has led to floors in department stores designed so that shoppers can see the back and front wall of the store, and thus orient themselves. Callison pioneered this approach with Nordstrom.

### Aspiration: Being Taken Care Of

What do women want? Or men? Or those who live their lives in the age of data processing where they are asked for their social security number more often each day than their name? The answer is that they want to be treated like the individuals they are.

Thus, a key part of hospitality is the ability to create situations in which people are treated specially, where they hear their names often, in the resonant tones of service. Similarly, they want their department store changing room or their hotel suite to be designed in a way that enhances the quality of their experience.

Hotel patrons, particularly those under forty who have seen very little personalized service in their lives, would like to have some. GenX wants a lobby that invites them to relax, pick up a magazine and have a waiter appear from the bar to ask them if they would like a glass of wine. And, it turns out, they don't care so much about having a big room as much as they want one that is thoughtfully designed, with remarkable materials and unexpected details.

### Wellness

Callison's focus on the creation of hospitable places meshes well with the patient-centered attitude toward the delivery of healthcare that has emerged over the last couple of decades. The firm has worked with numerous clients to create environments that are comfortable and familiar, reducing stress for patients and their families, and making it easier for patients to focus on getting well.

Callison's role in furthering the transition in the delivery of healthcare from a disease-focused model to a patient- and wellness-focused model coincides with the development of new technologies that have made it possible to create environments that no longer spotlight the apparatus of healing.

As the healthcare industry has become increasingly competitive, hospitals (and others) look for any advantage they can get — including the creation of hospitable environments that appeal to patients as consumers, a point of view that Callison is well equipped to provide.

Even the kinds of exterior touches that had proven so successful in hotel and shopping center design, such as elegant entrances, inviting public spaces and appropriate retail, have proven to be as welcoming and reassuring in a healthcare context as they are for other, less critical kinds of destinations.

### Convergence

Spoken or written, the word "hospitality" evokes a sense of warmth, welcome and home as surely as "hospital" still sends shivers up most spines. Ironically, both derive from the same medieval root "hospe" or "host." By translating design elements from its voluminous and varied four-decade hospitality practice to other fields, Callison is doing its part to put the words back in alignment, using design to help make the worlds of healthcare, as well as retail, office, and residential, a little more hospitable.

**PROVIDENCE HEALTH SYSTEM**
PROVIDENCE HEALTH CARE CENTER IS A PREMIER EXAMPLE OF THE SISTERS OF PROVIDENCE VISION, WHERE THE APPROACH TO HEALTHCARE DELIVERY FOCUSES ON EDUCATION, HEALTH-MAINTENANCE AND PRIMARY CARE, INTEGRATED WITH SPECIALTY CARE IN AN OUTPATIENT SETTING.

**WHISTLER DELTA LODGE**
THE RENOVATION OF WESTMONT HOSPITALITY'S DELTA LODGE AT WHISTLER RESORT INCLUDES UPGRADED STANDARDS AND A CHARACTER THAT IS MORE IN TUNE WITH ITS PACIFIC NORTHWEST SURROUNDINGS. THE DELTA LODGE OFFERS ENHANCED RETAIL TENANTS, UPGRADED PUBLIC AREAS AND NEW MEETING SPACE.

W HOTEL

SEATTLE, WASHINGTON

In Seattle, Callison created the first new W from the ground up, introducing the sophisticated design detail and inviting sense of place that set the standard for Starwood's boutique hotel brand.

The only totally new hotel brand to emerge in the last decade, "W" was created to capture the new wave of young, sophisticated business professionals who had emerged as trend leaders going into the twenty-first century.

Research had focused on the group widely referred to as GenX, and noted that these men and women in their twenties and thirties had grown up with an institutional sameness that had created a hunger for the sophisticated individual. This phenomenon explained the success of the small "boutique" hotels thriving in many American cities.

### Architecture with Personality

Completed in September 1999, the 325,000-square-foot, 435-room Seattle W was the first newly built hotel with more than 250 rooms in downtown Seattle since 1983. It brought to the city the chain's unique brand strategy: to have each hotel reflect the flavor and personality of its location, while having the sophistication and "nowness" that would become the W signature. Callison used its deep knowledge of Seattle's urban context to create a modern design to reflect the city's casual, hip, lifestyle with sensitivity to its strong architectural heritage.

# OTEL

With the site's extremely tight footprint challenging the hotel's public spaces, designers used architecture to create a sense of openness within the hotel. High ceilings and large windows that can open to the sidewalk give the building's relatively intimate lobby an expansive feeling. As a reflection of Pacific Northwest character, large windows connect the lobby, lounge and restaurant to street life. Corner guestrooms feature floor-to-ceiling windows framing spectacular city, bay, and mountain vistas.

Today, the W brand is a thriving part of the Starwood family with 19 hotels in some of the hipper cities around the world. The "W" stands for a lot of things ... warm, wonderful, witty, wired; and in Seattle, because of Callison's involvement, the "W" stands above all for welcome.

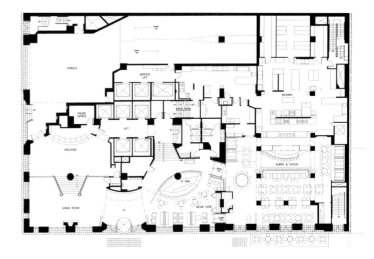

METROPOLITAN TOWER

SEATTLE, WASHINGTON

Located at the edge of Seattle's retail core rather than in one of its established downtown neighborhoods, the Metropolitan uses hospitality-inspired design and service to attract residents to its uptown address.

As Seattle's newest residential tower and the first highrise completed in Seattle following the 9/11/2001 attacks, the Metropolitan briefly held the spotlight as the test case to see if downtown highrise living was still viable. It was.

### Residential Project, Commercial Neighborhood

Since the Metropolitan Tower's uptown address stands apart from downtown Seattle's established residential districts, its location offered a point of distinction that could attract the growing number of people drawn to the bustle and amenities of the city. Flanked by office towers, upscale retail, restaurants, hotels and a new Federal courthouse, the location offered a mix of activities and uses.

### Gracious Living

The 24-story, 368-unit luxury apartment tower rests on a seven-story podium that includes parking and street-front retail. Its dramatic architectural profile encases 47 different unit floor plans, and the grand hotel style lobby sets the tone for amenities such as concierge and valet service, a full-service health club, business and conference center, guest suites and a spacious, eighth-floor garden terrace.

Residents ranging from their early 20s to mid-70s cite the array of services as well as proximity to social and work opportunities as reasons they chose to live there. Despite its completion amid a sharp economic decline and high-rise jitters, the building, when it opened, was nearly 90% leased.

T R O P O

# PROV

## PROVIDENCE HEALTH SYSTEM

ANCHORAGE, ALASKA    SNOHOMISH COUNTY, WASHINGTON

Smart healthcare
planning resulted
in a flexible,
efficient road map
for growth.

As Alaska's major healthcare institution, Providence Alaska Medical Center wanted
to upgrade and expand their facility to meet a wider range of patient needs. Goals
for the comprehensive five-year masterplan developed by Callison for the campus
were three-fold: to satisfy the immediate need for additional medical office space
and ambulatory patient services; to correct functional inefficiencies; and to
provide long-term flexibility.

For the first phase, a new five-story Medical Office Building was constructed over
an existing one-story neonatal intensive care unit and maternity unit with minimal
disruption to the hospital's day-to-day operations. In addition to the MOB, an
Outpatient Ambulatory Surgery was expanded and redesigned for improved delivery
of outpatient services.

ID E N C

Providence Health Care Center's less intimidating, more hospitable environment puts the emphasis on a wellness-based approach to healthcare.

At the time it was built, Providence Health Care Center, in Snohomish County, Washington, represented a new concept in healthcare delivery where the approach focuses on education, health maintenance and primary care integrated with specialty care in an outpatient setting. It is a setting conceived to support all the stakeholders in the healing process — patients, caregivers, families and physicians. This facility anticipated the managed care system by centralizing services through freestanding primary care delivery.

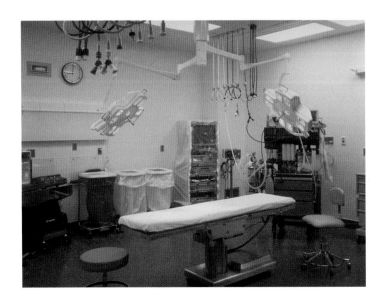

ST. CH

ST. CHARLES MEDICAL CENTER

BEND, OREGON

Since 1989, Callison has progressively transformed the setting for Central Oregon's St. Charles Medical Center to better support the hospital's holistic style of medicine and management, and its growing emphasis on health and wellness.

The comfort and convenience of patients was uppermost in Callison's plans for St. Charles. Features like soft bedding, indirect lighting, and 24-hour room service enhance physical comfort. Hospitable public areas, such as waiting rooms, the chapel and cafeteria, ease anxiety. A well-designed entryway leading to an elegant, comfortable lobby welcomes and reassures. While all of these might have been second nature in hotels and resorts, they remained largely unheard of in hospital design. Since the beginning of their collaboration in the late 1980s, Callison has worked with St. Charles to incorporate elements of sound, touch, taste, smell, and vision in the design of their facilities to create an experience that offers comfort, inspiration and empowerment.

### Health and Learning

St. Charles is and always has been an inpatient, acute-care institution, but in every step forward is moving to a position as a health and wellness place. The 2002 opening of the Center for Health and Learning served as a physical embodiment of this position. Envisioned as a community asset, the Center for Health and Learning was designed as a people-friendly, educational resource and venue that supports the healing environment.

ARLES

In the end, it was not by chance that a new kind of healing environment was taking shape at St. Charles. The institution is known nationally for its innovative approach to care and management, reflected in a philosophy of patient-centered care, holistic healing and wellness, and one that would naturally be inclined to help put hospitality back into hospital care.

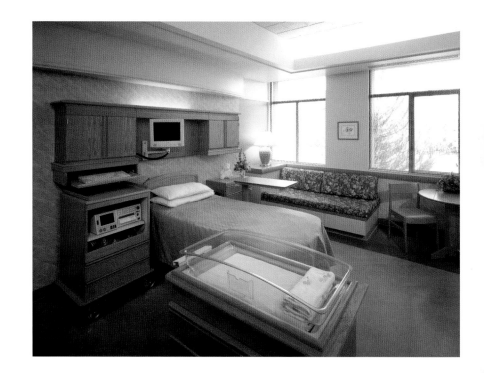

ST. FRANCIS HOSPITAL OUTPATIENT CENTER

With its new outpatient facility that gives patients and their families convenient access and privacy, volumes are up at St. Francis Hospital.

Like many community hospitals, St. Francis, one of the nation's Top 100 Hospitals, was facing increased competition in its fast-developing region. With its advanced surgical facilities and equipment and efficiencies gained by separating same-day surgery, the 62,500-square-foot Outpatient Center took aim at improving physician satisfaction and increasing throughput.

Callison carefully designed the facility to respect people's sense of privacy and convenience, with different entrances for surgical patients versus those in for radiation or other therapeutic services. There is always more than one person at the reception desk and patients or family members can consult in private cubicles. Color and furnishings echo the calm nature of the new healing garden located between the Outpatient Center and the hospital's patient wing.

ANCIS

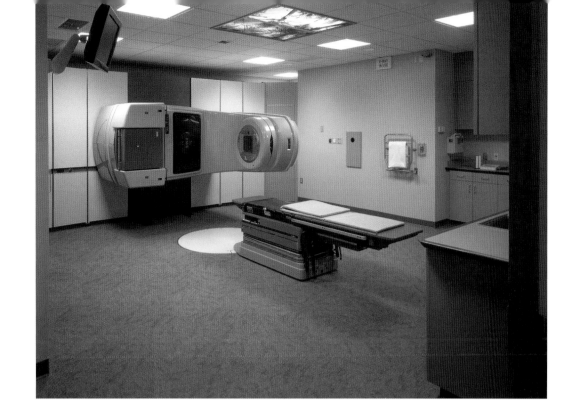

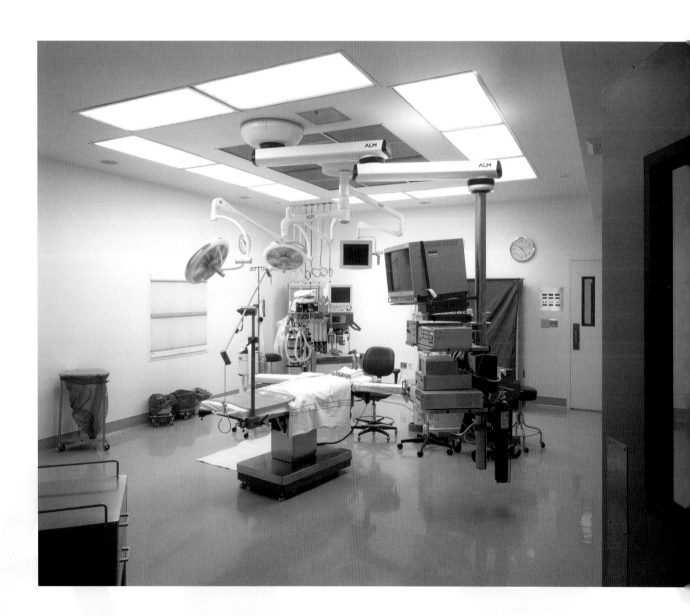

# BOEIN

SEATTLE, WASHINGTON

Drama and excitement help make these the last two pieces of the Pacific Science Center's transformation into a regional showcase for education and entertainment.

The Boeing Imax Theater has been nicknamed "the orb" because it is enclosed in an oblate spheroid that appears to float above the new glass gallery space. The organic shape made of high-tech materials and coatings references both the futuristic, high-tech aspect of science and the natural sciences. Callison, working with theater designer Denis Laming, was recognized for its design work for the Boeing Imax Theater, particularly the graphics, which have enhanced the entry and ticket-buying process and the lobby.

The Ackerley Family Exhibit Gallery and Tropical Butterfly House, located in the column-free glass structure, is home to Pacific Science Center's permanent tropical butterfly installation as well as a changing insect exhibit. It is a glass-clad, open space that encompasses the 4,000-square-foot Tropical Butterfly House at one end.

# GIMAX

## ACKERLEY FAMILY EXHIBIT GALLERY

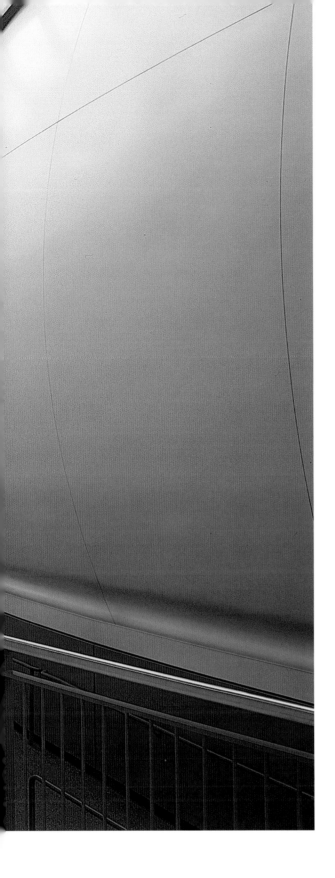

BOEING IMAX THEATER AND ACKERLEY FAMILY EXHIBIT GALLERY

PACIFIC SCIENCE CENTER

SEATTLE, WASHINGTON

In new and renovated buildings for Seattle's Pacific Science Center, a series of glass exhibit pavilions give the public a window on Science Center activities and views to its landmark arches.

The Pacific Science Center began life as a collection of windowless concrete cubes built for the 1962 Seattle International Exposition. During the 1990s, Callison, engaged as both masterplanner and designer, transformed those six cubes into the individual elements that have made the Pacific Science Center an exciting, world-class seat of science education and experience at the heart of the Seattle Center. Along with the neighboring Space Needle, this collection of theater, sports, cinema, amusement and museum venues is one of the nation's top five attractions.

The elements that make up the Pacific Science Center include the Willard W. Smith Planetarium, which was completed in 1992, the Technology Pavilion of 1994, the Discovery Lab of 1997, and the Boeing IMAX Theater, Ackerley Family Exhibit Gallery and the Tropical Butterfly House.

### Creating a Community Face

Essentially the same bare-boned boxes put up for the 1962 World's Fair, the complex did provide good flexible space for exhibitions, but did not adequately serve the Center's educational or scientific uses. Nor did it fit into the aspirations of the Center to become a "world-class" scientific and educational institution or provide the visibility required for national and international recognition.

As a community-based organization, the complex needed to be physically refocused outward toward the community rather than inward-looking as they had been designed for the fair.

Prior to the renovation, for example, the Technology Pavilion only allowed entry from the Fairgrounds at Seattle Center. The complex was open only to the north, with essentially blank facades facing the other directions. A new window wall on the city side provides a new public entrance, and exciting views of the exhibits inside. This "opening up" also solved a primary functional problem: providing a drop-off for the 80,000 school children who visit each year. Creating a new drop off point provided direct, secure access that also offers weather-protected queuing space. The canopy design carefully followed the highly technological structural elements presented in the original building.

# WE

## WESTIN WESTMINSTER

WESTMINSTER, COLORADO

Since opening in April 2000, the Westin has won kudos from numerous travel services and publications as the best hotel in the Westminster area, and among Greater Denver's elite hospitality establishments.

Like its nearby Callison-designed neighbor, FlatIron Crossing, the 300-room Westin Westminster uses a contemporary design to reflect the setting and lifestyle of the Rockies. Set on a lake, midway between Denver and Boulder in the rapidly growing town of Westminster, the site also includes a nature preserve and wetlands.

### Homage to the Rocky Mountain Lifestyle

The Westin's peaked roof, braced overhangs, and rustic rock pilings pay homage to the rugged and beautiful landscape outside, while inside the warm stone and wood of the lobby establishes an atmosphere of casual sophistication and hospitality. With its "resort" setting, Westin Westminster is not only a unique destination for business lodging and conferencing, but also a recreational and entertainment draw for locals and tourists. Its relaxed style provides a counterpoint to the emerging high-tech environments surrounding the Front Range.

### A Mixed-Use Destination

The Westin is one element of a planned mixed-use destination that today includes a conference center owned by the City of Westminster. The site also contains a community center for use by Westminster residents, a skating rink, and retail and dining elements. Twin office buildings are also planned in order to attract one or more corporate headquarters, and transform the site into a true mixed-use live, work and play destination.

Because of the public/private nature of the project, Callison worked closely with planners from the town of Westminster to integrate the conference and community center into the design. At the same time, Callison was able to adjust certain elements of the project to the new requirements that arose when the Westin hotel chain was acquired by Starwood Hotel and Resorts in 2000.

# TETO

## TETON CLUB

JACKSON HOLE, WYOMING

With its strong connections to the land and five-star level of design and service, the Teton Club attracts a new breed of buyers to the lucrative residential resort industry.

### The Focal Point

Developed jointly by Raintree Resorts International, Inc. of Dallas, Texas, and the Jackson Hole Mountain Resort, the Teton Club is a resort destination and the focal point of a new residential community, pedestrian promenade and commercial center.

A relatively new concept "fractional" resort at the foot of the Jackson Hole, Wyoming, ski area, the Teton Club consists of forty two- and three-bedroom luxury units ranging in size from 1,200 to 1,800 square feet.

### Design Imperatives

The Teton Club also responds to the design challenges inherent in building a ski resort; for example, a sloped site. The C-shaped footprint respects the dictates of the site, showcasing the vistas outside its doors at the same time as it allows for the accommodations and amenities that give the project its resort hotel ambience. Another design requirement is the need to deal with large volumes of snow. In order to minimize the risk of dangerous snow loads, architectural features such as gables and benches were designed to either shed snow or allow it to collect where there is no danger.

N CLUB

### Designed Like a Five-Star Hotel

What separates the Teton Club from other condo-style vacation homes is that the design, amenities and management are more in the mode of a five-star resort. All spaces are furnished and decorated with the finest natural materials, elegant and comfortable furniture and handcrafted details, from the units to the hardwood-lined ski locker room and full-service health club. As in luxury resorts, hospitality elements include room service, concierge and housekeeping services available around the clock.

SEMI

THE INN AT SEMIAHMOO

BLAINE, WASHINGTON

A seaside resort rising from the vestiges of an abandoned cannery, the Inn at Semiahmoo offers guests an experience that is as informal and luxurious as the scenery that surrounds it.

The Inn at Semiahmoo is a four-star waterfront resort hotel set at the end of a mile-long sand spit on Puget Sound near the Canadian border. The site was formerly the home of the Alaska Packers Cannery, a complex of by then shuttered structures that for decades had given that area of coastline a ruggedly handsome visual context.

In the late 1980s, Callison was hired by the developer Atlas Hotels to develop an adaptive reuse design to renovate some of the existing cannery buildings along with new construction, resulting in a 200-room hotel that would include 3,600 square feet of meeting rooms, a 7,000-square-foot ballroom, 30,000 square feet of recreation facilities, restaurants and lounges.

Despite severe time and budget constraints, the goal was to create a luxury destination at which guests could stroll along unspoiled sand dunes, play golf in a spectacular setting or work in the unhurried, uncluttered atmosphere of the Inn.

AH M O

## Complementing Nature

The project's design goal was to reflect and enhance the integrity of a place rich in tradition and natural beauty. The design addressed these considerations through large simple massing that referenced the existing cannery buildings and a low horizontal profile that complemented the special qualities of the sand spit. At the same time, the hotel's design encouraged relaxation, providing walkways, vistas and water activities enabling guests to enjoy the natural beauty of the Pacific Northwest.

Completed in 1987, the Inn at Semiahmoo has earned both local and regional AIA honor awards.

# VILL

## VILLAGE AT MAMMOTH

MAMMOTH LAKES, CALIFORNIA

**This mixed-use resort village sets a new standard in the ski resort industry by creating a town center that meets the shopping and entertainment needs of both resort visitors and year-round residents.**

The trend in resort development is to add retail and entertainment to the residential component. But, the focus has been primarily to extend the guest stay or provide more recreational opportunities. At the Village at Mammoth, the market for the retail village extends beyond the 265 residential units to the 7,000 residents of the Town of Mammoth Lakes. Callison designed the village at the base of Mammoth Mountain to give the town a new center.

The Village plan organizes the 75,000 square feet of retail along two streets. The resort's multistory lodges surround three pedestrian plazas all linked by one of the streets. The plaza that houses the gondola lift to the mountain is the Village's main gathering spot. Another plaza centers the lively restaurant and nightlife zone that attracts visitors and locals. A third open space is a quiet, serene setting that offers a place to get away from it all, or to try fly-fishing in the pond. Together, they enhance the resort destination and activate the community year-round. The second retail street, which fronts the California State Highway's access to the Mammoth Mountain Base Station, offers a tenant and service mix oriented more to the community.

The Village is designed with layers of meaning that place it in the town and landscape as if built over time. It is a town with "story" that creates meaningful connections to the community and fits thoughtfully into its environment. It is a destination reminiscent of the grand lodges and craftsmen design of the past, with a contemporary expression.

# PUTTING THE OFFICE TO WORK
## Using Corporate Real Estate to Reduce Costs and Boost Performance

**The ongoing pursuit and application of the kind of design intelligence that transforms business space into a working asset has taken Callison and its clients to remarkable new places.**

One of Callison's great strengths, and most satisfying achievements, is the enduring nature of its relationships with industry pioneers like Boeing, Microsoft, Hewlett-Packard and Washington Mutual. Many of these relationships were established during the firm's formative years, when it became clear that Callison's propensity for evaluating its clients against the backdrop of market trends made the firm atypical in the lengths to which it went to make sure the clients were getting both what they wanted and needed.

There was something about Callison's mastery of space that made it more viable and valuable. This was not an accident. With a firm bias toward business, Callison strove to make all of its designs contributors to corporate cost savings and to make the real estate a key factor in a company's creativity, productivity and profitability.

### Real Estate as an Asset

Putting a company's real estate to work was a knack Callison had honed in the retail arena; a skill the firm had been able to transfer to its corporate office practice. In retail, there was little choice, a store had to work for its owners at, for example, being its own billboard. If the design of the store did not communicate its purpose, brand and desirability in a heartbeat, that business wouldn't last amid stores that did.

Callison's assertion was that corporate real estate not only could, but for the sake of competitiveness, would have to relate directly to that company's business objectives in much the same way that retail space did. When that connection between work setting and corporate goals was made, the office outgrew its reputation as a necessary but profit-gobbling place to warehouse workers.

Instead, the physical space of a company, one of the biggest investments that businesses make, could be configured to serve as a dynamic facilitator of creativity, commitment and drive. Comfortable, compelling workspaces were similarly a bottom-line enhancer able to provide a powerful incentive to catch and keep the most talented and driven employee.

**HEWLETT PACKARD BUILDING 20**
HEWLETT PACKARD'S NEW WORK SETTING AT
HEADQUARTERS ACHIEVES AGGRESSIVE SQUARE-
FOOT-PER-PERSON RATIOS BY PROVIDING A SERIES
OF ANCILLARY AREAS DESIGNED TO SUPPORT THE
VARIOUS TASKS PERFORMED DURING A TYPICAL
WORKDAY. A MAJORITY OF THE WORKSTATIONS
ARE "FREE ADDRESS," PROVIDED AT A PERCENTAGE
OF THE TOTAL NUMBER OF WORKERS.

## Walking the Talk

So convinced was Callison that the path of paying real estate was the right one, that it dedicated considerable staff time and resources investigating and, equally important, getting the message out about innovative ways to increase the business power of design.

Ultimately Callison assembled a group of executives from various design-related companies to challenge the deeply rooted corporate stereotype of "the office." The team studied social, economic, and environmental and technology trends that were influencing the way people lived and worked.

The result was the sponsorship of an exhibit called Future@Work in which Callison's workplace study initiatives took corporeal form. Opening in 1997 and housed for three years on the twenty-eighth floor of Seattle's Columbia Seafirst Center, Future@Work was a 5,000-square-foot brief for the utilization of advanced workplace design in the name of enhanced creativity, performance and competitive advantage.

Future@Work also proved to be a powerful tool that communicated in tangible and readily understandable ways, Callison's own excitement at the new workplace paradigm.

Today, the exhibit lab think-tank/educational center/showroom and larger-than-life office design sketchpad that is Future@Work has morphed to incorporate the findings gleaned from some 6,000 visitors and myriad client projects.

**WELLS FARGO/RAGEN MACKENZIE**
WHEN WELLS FARGO AND RAGEN MACKENZIE MERGED THEIR SPECIALTY BUSINESSES OF PRIVATE BANKING AND INVESTMENT BANKING, CALLISON WAS CALLED ON TO HELP UNITE THE DISTINCT CULTURES THROUGH NEW OFFICE DESIGN.

## Curious Callison

As important as Future@Work is as a component of Callison's ongoing office design program, it is just as important as an expression of the firm's commitment to exploration, idea generation and change — all in the service of client needs and business objectives. This rigorously curious side of Callison is a characteristic that has become even more valuable in helping its clients prosper in an increasingly complex global marketplace.

## Measuring Returns

Meanwhile, nearly a decade into the work, Callison's studies are becoming workplace benchmarks. The design initiatives that sparked Future@Work have taken on important lives of their own. What a decade-and-a-half ago were interesting Callison theories about the use of space as a business tool, are now becoming business better practices.

The investments that clients are making in pilot programs to gather data that would measure changes in performance due to the impact of Callison innovations in workplace design is a testament to the firm's success both in space design and in communicating the message.

**KEY CENTER**
LOCATED IN DOWNTOWN BELLEVUE, WASHINGTON, KEY CENTER'S CREATIVE CONCRETE CORE DESIGN ALLOWS FOR LARGE, FLEXIBLE FLOOR PLATES, EFFICIENT LOAD FACTORS, INCREASED CEILING HEIGHTS, UNOBSTRUCTED VIEWS — EVEN EXTRA MANEUVERING ROOM IN THE GARAGE.

**KCPQ BROADCAST STUDIO**
IN MOVING TO A CONVERTED FACTORY ON SEATTLE'S LAKE UNION, KCPQ SOUGHT A HIGHER PROFILE IN ITS MAJOR MARKET. IN CONTRAST TO THE TYPICAL "FORTRESS" DESIGN USED FOR MOST TV STATIONS, KCPQ WANTED A FRIENDLY PRESENCE THAT EMBODIED A REGIONAL STYLE, WITHOUT SACRIFICING SECURITY.

MICR

MICROSOFT WORLD HEADQUARTERS

REDMOND, WASHINGTON

When Callison began collaborating with Microsoft in the early 1980s, the software startup considered its three 60,000-square-foot buildings a slightly extravagant amount of space. Over nine million square feet later, Microsoft is still growing at an unprecedented pace.

Callison began providing architectural services for Microsoft's World Headquarters in 1984 and since then has designed over three million square feet of facilities for research, design, marketing, administrative and distribution functions. Over the years, Callison's goal has been to design the campus to reflect Microsoft's understated corporate image, provide for the software giant's long-term needs and create a user-oriented campus environment. The unobtrusive architecture and rich landscaping create informal, collegiate-like surroundings while maintaining the natural beauty of the site.

OSOFT

EDDIE BAUER CORPORATE HEADQUARTERS

REDMOND, WASHINGTON

Under its rainfly-inspired roof, the corporate home for Eddie Bauer brings staff together in an elegant expression of the company's down-to-earth culture of function and quality.

In 1920, a young Seattle merchant opened a store called Eddie Bauer's Sports Shop and made a pledge: "To give you such outstanding quality, value, service, and guarantee that we may be worthy of your high esteem." Seventy-seven years later, the company called simply Eddie Bauer had become a $1.5 billion business.

In line with its nearly eighty-year tradition, the company sought something for its corporate headquarters beyond the ordinary, a space that would resonate with the company's woodsy ethos and low-keyed culture.

### Under One Roof

For years the company's growth had been managed by simply leasing new space around Redmond, Washington. By the late 1990s, Eddie Bauer employees were spread out across multiple locations and management decided it was time to bring everyone together under one roof. Callison dived deeply into the client's culture and then emerged with an essence that would be represented through elegant and appropriate design.

D I E

The goal to house both corporate management and product development teams in a single location called for highly flexible office space that could expand and contract with shifts in market demand. The functional elements of the design were divided to form irregular and informal spaces, varying in both materials and the amount of glass. Over 700 feet long, the building's facade is stepped and angled, decreasing the visual mass and introducing more light into the interior. Capping the building is the highly distinctive "floating roof," inspired by a rainfly.

Inside the headquarters are layers of Pacific Northwest symbols and references to the Eddie Bauer tradition. These include basic Bauer product colors, filtered daylight, rough slate, fir, weathered metal and the company's own furniture products. Outside, numerous walkways and terraces were used to further break down building scale. Integration with the natural setting was accomplished by landscaping that brought foliage into close proximity with the enclosed spaces.

# FUT

FUTURE@WORK

SEATTLE, WASHINGTON

More than 6,000 leaders from business, academia and government have experienced the power of real estate through Future@Work, a ground-breaking exhibit designed to show companies how to sustain business, people and the environment through innovative workplace strategies.

### Transforming Business Real Estate into an Asset

The impetus for Future@Work was a series of meetings in 1995 among executives of design and architecture-related companies. The goal was to find solutions for what they saw as the growing gap between the new kinds of work imperatives decreed by the information economy and the early 20th-century environments in which most of that work was done. The corollary was that corporate real estate could, if thought about and utilized in the correct ways, be a powerful tool to enhance both corporate creativity and profitability.

### Show Not Tell

In 1996, Callison as part of "The Office of the Future Consortium," developed a space that would be the new kind of workplace, where tomorrow and today's work could be most efficiently done. The space would serve a multitude of purposes. It would be a place where new ideas could be "shown," not just "told." It would be a marketing center for new products, a lab for workplace research, an exhibit, an educational center, and an exceptionally comfortable place for people to meet and share ideas.

URE

## An Office Space unlike Any Other

Called Future@Work, this 5,000-square-foot showcase, lab, exhibition and meeting place located on the 28th floor of Seattle's Columbia Seafirst Center, was quite unlike any workspace that had been seen before. Combining the newest, best thinking in design fields such as technology, lighting, sustainability, social anthropology, graphics, media, engineering and infrastructure development, Future@Work addressed workspace related issues simple and complex.

One key theme that resonated throughout Future@Work was that business space should always be designed for more than a single use. In the exhibit, a boardroom table built to be dismantled in seconds would be replaced by movable work "pods," enabling a meeting space to be quickly transformed into a office space, or a studio, or reception room. Future@Work was full of spaces with utility factors two, three, four and more times those of a traditional single-use workspace.

## A Second Life

The success of Future@Work, and its capacity as a tool to communicate workplace ideas to non-design-trained executives, led the Consortium to take Future@Work and transform it. In its second incarnation, 2,800 square feet on the 15th floor of the City Centre building where the firm has its offices, Future@Work is a permanent part of the Callison "show-not-tell" toolbox, and a much sought-after meeting and brainstorming space. It is also the place where designers can spend a few moments to recharge and commune with what clearly is the future of work at work. Future@Work is a tangible expression of Callison's commitment to exploration, idea generation and change.

LA

LATHAM & WATKINS

ORANGE COUNTY, CALIFORNIA

When Callison turned its first project with this California-based law firm into a case study of how interior design can save a firm money, they ended up with a relationship that has lasted more than nine years and a dozen projects worldwide.

### Starting Small

The case study in point: Prove how a redesign budget could be more usefully spent reconfiguring this law firm's back office space, which could be enhanced for increased efficiency and cost savings.

Latham & Watkins gave Callison the difficult task of providing space for increased staffing and doing it within the parameters of the firm's existing Orange County offices. By dedicating space to more than one use, and creating smaller but more elegant and efficient offices, Callison was able to make room for more employees, keep existing staff members happy while increasing access to daylight and improving lighting and furnishings.

# T H A M

EXIT

**SOF**

SOFTIMAGE

SANTA MONICA, CALIFORNIA

An early example of the firm's visionary approach to office design, the headquarters for Hollywood animator SoftImage took the idea of "more for less" to a new level.

In 1995, SoftImage, one of the pioneers of digital 3-D animation and motion capture software, required a workspace in which it could concentrate its engineers and artists. The company was working on a number of Hollywood projects with companies like Sony Pictures, Industrial Light & Magic, Image Works and others and needed an office that would reinforce their creative process and growing status.

A building was found in Santa Monica, only ten thousand square feet, but a space that was in line with the work and cash flow. The problem was that the Montreal-headquartered company not only needed space to house its employees, but also required a large open area to use as a motion-capture studio. Callison was hired to see if all the required uses could be shoehorned in.

Just in the start-up phase of the self-funded office space initiative that would lead to the Future@Work exhibit, Callison was far ahead of the design curve in promoting and designing office space that lowered both cost and required square footage by designing space for multiple uses, as in the case of SoftImage, into a motion-capture studio. Using rolling "pod" workstations, office space could be transformed into the studio in a matter of minutes by simply rolling them out of the way. There was an added benefit as well. When the motion-capture studio was not in use, teams could arrange the pods in any configuration that suited them.

TIMA

ORRICK

# ORRICK, HERRINGTON & SUTCLIFFE, LLP

SEATTLE, WASHINGTON    MENLO PARK, CALIFORNIA

# Innovative planning and comfortable design helps Orrick, Herrington & Sutcliffe maximize their workspace.

When San Francisco–based law firm Orrick, Herrington & Sutcliffe, LLP expanded into the Seattle market, they wanted a workplace that enhanced employee interaction and expressed a multicultural character with an emphasis on warmth and comfort.

Design of the 48,000-square-foot branch office created a Pacific Rim aesthetic by breaking down barriers and giving access to views, by the use of wood and glass throughout the office and by the introduction of inviting group spaces. A bold yet simple cantilevered stair visible from shared communal spaces promotes communication between floors and a "village green," located at the heart of the space and filled with movable furniture, data/power connections and plasma screen symbolically unites the floors. To maximize the time of visitors, a client lounge provides a dedicated space where clients can work while waiting.

The office's crisp, elegant aesthetic serves as an excellent backdrop to stunning views of Puget Sound and the firm's compelling collection of painting, photography and sculpture.

## Variety

This was the solution for Orrick, Herrington & Sutcliffe to maximize space in its 43,000-square-foot Silicon Valley office. Through a plan that included a variety of spaces for collaborating, private work or simply taking a break, Callison accommodated doubling the number of offices to meet expected growth with a workplace designed to reflect the firm's collaborative attitude.

Valuable square footage was carved out for meeting spaces that still achieves a maximum number of offices, compensating for the smaller spaces with offices that are more comfortable and with angled walls and appropriately scaled, flexible furnishings. A consolidated Conference Center houses client meeting areas as well as a multipurpose space for socializing, the "village green" for collaboration or just as an alternative work venue and an on-site dining area that can also handle large group meetings. These add to the variety of options.

Translating this client's progressive and fluid style into a design theme that centered around the serene, changing qualities of water, inspired solutions that also helped lessen the space constraints. For example, an interior glass wall created along the main circulation route amplified the amount of natural light coming into the core office space.

# BOEIN

## BOEING CUSTOMER SERVICE TRAINING CENTER

Boeing's training center integrates highly sophisticated technology with a student-friendly environment to provide world-class flight instruction.

Boeing Commercial Airplane Group's Customer Service Training Center was designed to train pilots and maintenance crews from airlines throughout the world. The 600,000-square-foot center's plan includes classrooms, flight simulators, technology and physiology labs, a video studio, conference facilities and athletic and food service facilities.

**The Goal**

One of the challenges was that the facility is used by an international clientele, so the layout had to be instantly understandable to students from diverse cultural backgrounds and languages.

As many as 800 students come to the Customer Service Training Center each month, in addition to 1,100 instructors and support staff from Boeing, to find a technically superior learning environment within a functional, efficient and budget-oriented facility.

G CUST

# SPECIAL DELIVERY
## Design Delivery Systems that Meet Business Needs

To handle the architectural production needs for major clients worldwide, Callison combines the strengths of robust delivery systems, industry savvy and diverse geographic experience. The single-source accountability that clients receive from using one firm for both design and implementation results in relevant design, efficiently delivered.

Whether it's the implementation of highly complex, one-of-a-kind projects or the roll-out of prototype designs on a very rapid, geographically diverse basis, it takes a rare breed of design firm to do both.

As much time, energy and creativity as Callison devotes to its highest level of design, it gives in equal measure to creating new and often unorthodox delivery mechanisms that respond to a client's needs and market expectations.

### Smarter Practices
The Callison passion for designing "Smarter Places" has its delivery corollary in the development of what might be called "Smarter Practices" — a constantly evolving toolbox of systems for the management of project delivery. Every new project that comes to Callison is looked at in terms of finding better, faster and more efficient ways of getting a building or a program up and online. No matter how big or how small the project, no matter where it is located or how many are contemplated, Callison understands that the faster a project gets built, the better it is for the client's business.

### High Volume, High Speed, High Savings
Because speed and accuracy are paramount to the successful delivery of architectural projects, which are inherently complex and sensitive to market conditions, Callison has created processes flexible enough to enable customization and rigorous enough to maintain efficiency. Over the last decade, Callison has worked with clients such as Washington Mutual, Cingular Wireless, Pottery Barn and Pottery Barn Kids, Williams Sonoma, Cole Haan, Trish McEvoy, Gap, Verizon Wireless and Guess to evolve such systems that help them meet their business goals.

## Matching Callison's Organization With the Clients'

Businesses that use architectural services frequently divide their management of the procurement process into two distinct portions led by two different parts of the organization: one group focused on developing new concepts aimed at furthering strategic business goals (Design) and the other on assuring that the resulting design solutions are implemented (Construction). Callison has mirrored this in its own organization, building a large, dedicated production team to work with design and prototyping—all under the same architectural roof.

Like its implementation-minded counterparts in the client organization who measure success by how well they met or exceeded time and budget milestones for expansion, Callison focuses its production mindset on efficiency, cost-effectiveness and volume-oriented logistics.

One example of Callison's understanding of the impact of savings over time came during the roll-out of bank branches in early 2003. Callison saved the client more than $500,000 in copying and shipping

COLE HAAN

CALLISON AND COLE HAAN'S IN-HOUSE DESIGN TEAM COLLABORATED TO REVITALIZE AND ENHANCE THE EXISTING MID-CENTURY MODERN DESIGN OF THE COLE HAAN PROTOTYPE STORE. THE CONCEPT WAS REDEFINED TO CREATE A STRONGER BRAND IDENTITY AND EFFICIENCIES FOR THE FUTURE ROLLOUT OF NEW STORES.

costs by reducing the size of drawings so that they could be faxed rather than special-messengered to sites. By relocating an electrical outlet in a prototype design, Callison was able to save the client $1,500 per branch. With over 1,000 branches planned, the savings totaled $1.5 million.

## High Complexity, High Results

"Smarter Practices" have also made it possible to accomplish one-off projects in a fraction of the time convention allows — like the jet-speed delivery of the Boeing World Headquarters in Chicago, a fourteen-month project conceptualized and delivered in an unprecedented five months. If the "Book of Standard Design Delivery" said it couldn't be done, Callison simply threw the book away and wrote a new one. And it took smarter practices such as intense collaboration strategies, customized tools and parallel processes to speed every aspect of delivery, from site-selection through move-in.

Trailblazing new project delivery territory is a challenge Callison welcomes. Many large design firms, spread out in multiple offices, can take weeks or even months to assemble a team for a project. A key to the success of the Boeing project was understanding the executives' initiatives, and having the resources at hand to assemble the right team, move quickly and coordinate with the more than 70 different companies that ultimately had a hand in the project. Callison's depth of expertise, concentrated in Seattle, enables the firm to form and reform groups, teams and taskforces to match a project's complexity.

**BOEING WORLD HEADQUARTERS**
CALLISON PARTICIPATED IN A THREE-DAY, THREE-CITY, SIXTY-BUILDING TOUR TO ASSIST THE BOEING COMPANY IN SELECTING THE SITE FOR ITS NEW WORLD HEADQUARTERS. THE FINAL PROJECT INCLUDES WORK SPACE FOR 500 EMPLOYEES AND A TWO-STORY BROADCAST STUDIO AND PRESSROOM. CALLISON RELIED ON COLLABORATIVE TEAMING AND INNOVATIVE APPROACHES IN THEIR ROLE OF DESIGN AND DOCUMENTATION.

**WAVVE TELECOMMUNICATIONS**
THIS ULTRA-SECURE, GLOBAL NETWORK OPERATIONS CENTER (GNOC) AND TELECOM CO-LOCATION FACILITY PROVIDES MANAGED SERVICES SOLUTIONS TO THE HIGH-TECH INDUSTRY. BUILT ON A FAST-TRACK SCHEDULE, THE PROJECT WAS DESIGNED AND CONSTRUCTED IN FIVE MONTHS.

## Accomplishing the Impossible

The benefit of having all the relevant resources located together to complement each other and draw on common experiences and expertise has proven to be a major benefit for companies that need fast and accurate research, design and documentation. It's what allows Callison to innovate mechanisms to deliver, on time and within budget, high-volume roll-outs and highly complex projects all over the world, accomplishing goals that others have deemed impossible.

**WASHINGTON MUTUAL**

OVER THE PAST TEN YEARS, WASHINGTON MUTUAL HAS GROWN TO BECOME ONE OF THE LARGEST FINANCIAL SERVICES COMPANIES IN THE UNITED STATES. SINCE STARTING OUT ON A SMALL NUMBER OF COMMUNITY BANKS IN 1989 DURING THE EARLY DAYS OF WASHINGTON MUTUAL'S NATIONWIDE EXPANSION, CALLISON'S RELATIONSHIP HAS GROWN IN MAGNITUDE AND MULTITUDE. SINCE THEN, CALLISON HAS DELIVERED MORE THAN FIVE MILLION SQUARE FEET OF WASHINGTON MUTUAL FACILITIES INCLUDING CORPORATE OFFICE SPACE, CAMPUS MASTER PLANNING, DATA CENTERS AND MORE THAN 1,500 RETAIL BANK ROLL-OUT PROJECTS NATIONWIDE.

WITH ITS RAPID GROWTH FUELED BY A BUSINESS STRATEGY TO PROVIDE A HIGHER LEVEL OF PERSONALIZED SERVICE THAN THEIR COMPETITORS, WASHINGTON MUTUAL SETS AN EXAMPLE OF BEST-IN-CLASS CUSTOMER SERVICE THAT RESONATES WITH CALLISON'S OWN. THROUGH ITS PRACTICE OF PROVIDING CUSTOMIZED DELIVERY SOLUTIONS THAT TARGET A CLIENT'S BUSINESS GROWTH DEMANDS, CALLISON HAS BEEN ABLE TO SUSTAIN A STRONG LEVEL OF SERVICE TO SUPPORT WASHINGTON MUTUAL.

**BO**

BOEING COMPANY WORLD HEADQUARTERS

CHICAGO, ILLINOIS

By marshalling the resources and talent necessary to design and construct 275,000 square feet of sophisticated office space, 1,700 miles away in just 117 days, Boeing redefined the promise of jet-speed delivery.

In late March 2001, Boeing Chairman and CEO Phil Condit startled the business world by announcing that the Boeing headquarters staff would be relocating out of the Puget Sound area to a "new, leaner corporate center more central to Boeing global operations, customers and financial markets." Condit explained the move in terms of the absolute requirement for Boeing to be "nimble and flexible." He neatly illustrated what those "turn on a dime" qualities meant for Boeing by noting that the company had not yet decided which of three possible finalist headquarter locations, Denver, Dallas/Fort Worth or Chicago, would be chosen.

### Nimbleness and Flexibility

Nimbleness and flexibility in the face of short notice were also very much on the minds of the design team as they thought about the Boeing relocation. Time was of the essence because the request had gone out from the Boeing chairman that the facility had to be chosen, designed, built and ready to occupy by the first week in September so employees could be moved and homes established by the time children returned to school.

Although the schedule was unprecedented, the project team of construction, design and other consultants assembled by Boeing was not taken by surprise, for Boeing was known for continuously challenging itself and its people to design and build airplanes that flew higher, farther, faster and more safely.

E I N G

The Boeing challenge to do something in design and construction that had never been done before was very much on the minds of Callison as work began. Callison's role in the buildout was design and documentation, and the Callison members of the project team found the challenge bracing: "To satisfy a schedule as unprecedented as this one," one designer recalled, "we knew we were not only going to have to throw away the book, but write an entirely new one."

## Design Before Acquisition?

The first chapter would focus on the question of how much of the planning and design work could be accomplished even before the city and site were selected. Quite a bit as it turned out. While Boeing and its major contractors, Callison and Turner, winnowed down potential sites — at the end of three days, it was down to 18 — the design team in Seattle began with early elements such as programming, researching furniture, assembling color palettes and procuring critical long-lead-time elements. Due to Callison's somewhat unorthodox, but successful reengineering of the typical space planning/test fit process, this was possible.

## 117 Days, 1,700 Miles

On May 10, Boeing announced that a 275,000-square-foot space on twelve floors of a downtown Chicago highrise at 100 N. Riverside had been chosen. That afternoon, a project office was set up in Chicago while simultaneously the team working on the Boeing project in Seattle was increased fivefold. Meanwhile, the Boeing inhouse consultant team began establishing the criteria for such things as audio-visual, information technology, food service and security, while Callison engaged an eleven-member consultant team including structural, mechanical, electrical and code experts. Ultimately, the project would entail the collaboration of more than 70 companies, not including vendors.

How do you create a team large enough to handle a vast workload, yet nimble enough for quick response? Three words: leadership, autonomy and partnering. To streamline what could have been a very complex decision-making process, designated project directors from Boeing, Callison and Turner, under the overall direction of Boeing, focused on frequent, action-oriented communication. Since meetings and troubleshooting occupied much of the day, design and drawing took place after hours, either at the onsite field office, which was staffed seven days a week for the duration of the project, or in Callison and Boeing Seattle offices. Boeing and Callison staff worked two shifts to support Turner crews working three shifts.

### Fueled by Collaborative Spirit

On September 5, 2001, Boeing began operations of its new world headquarters in Chicago, picking up exactly where it had left off the Friday before in Seattle, Washington. A sense of accomplishment, relief and sheer amazement ruled the day. In just 117 days, the Boeing, Callison and Turner team had been able to plan, design and construct 275,000 square feet of space, 1,700 miles away in Boeing's new Chicago home. Team structure, a 24/7 commitment and re-engineered design process aside, all agree that success hinged on the extraordinary effort of every member of the team and an uncommon spirit of cooperation among the hundreds of professionals dedicated to getting the job done.

BOEING COMPANY WORLD HEADQUARTERS

CINGULAR WIRELESS

MULTIPLE LOCATIONS, UNITED STATES

Designed to change the way consumers think, purchase and interact with wireless services and products, the new store prototype for Cingular Wireless increased sales by an average of 24%.

In 2001, Callison was working with client Cingular Wireless to create a new customer-friendly in-store wireless buying experience. To make sure that Cingular's branding message was unified across every aspect of the store experience, Callison worked directly with Cingular's public relations and advertising consultant.

### A New Wireless Buying Experience

Cingular's message "celebrating self-expression" that was brought to life in its ads, faced a three-dimensional challenge when planning for a retail store roll-out. With a new kind of store and a new, easy and fun way to try and buy wireless products, Cingular had an opportunity to redefine how the wireless industry approaches the store; and, as a new brand, a clean slate on which to present their message.

ULAR

To create a truly different buying experience, Cingular and Callison took a new look at metrics and devised unprecedented experiential goals married to critical aspects of the brand: to enrich the customer experience at a level that would engender customer loyalty; to differentiate Cingular from its competition through high-touch design; and to provide a shopping experience able to generate excitement and fun.

The expression of these goals in three-dimensional form is found in such elements as the Live Bar, an internet café-type element featuring live phones, accessories, wireless data devices, E-store and touch screens for customers to plug and play; the Express Checkout and Service and softer, warmer, humanistic lighting and design.

NOW FEATURING

cingula
WIREL

live
bar

Think of it as the
self-expression buffet.

Phone
a friend

Send an
Interactive Message

Test out the Wireless Internet

Check out Cingular.com

Express
yourself!

Cingular Wireless Calling Plans

FEDEX WORLD SERVICE CENTERS

MULTIPLE LOCATIONS, UNITED STATES

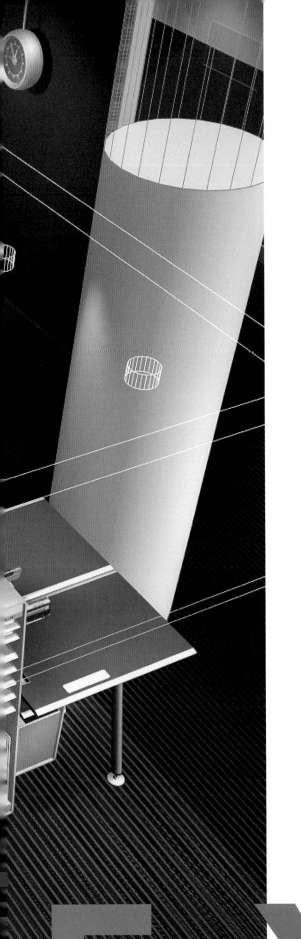

The prototype for FedEx's World Service Centers was developed to improve the company's brand image, customer experience and agent efficiency.

During the past two years, FedEx, with the help of outside consultants, conducted research to identify how FedEx is viewed in the marketplace, how it compares to its competition and what the key areas of focus should be for a new solution to its current World Service Centers.

Based on the initial research and preliminary prototype studies, Callison developed a new concept that will be tested in four FedEx World Service Centers in the Chicago area.

The design creates a new brand image that is distinctly FedEx, while addressing the needs of various customer types, complex operational requirements and diverse site conditions. The design language delivers consistent appearance, enhances interaction and reinforces FedEx's brand equity.

# WHAT'S NEXT FOR RETAIL
## Driving the Trends that Change the Face of Retail

Recognized as the world's number one retail design firm, Callison has been involved in creating, repositioning and occasionally doctoring some of the world's most recognizable retail destinations as well as the brands that complete them.

### Understanding the Changing Customer

Since Callison embarked on the business of designing for retail over twenty-five years ago, the old maxim that "the only thing that's constant is change" is as true today as it was then. In retail, change can come so quickly that not only will a prediction be proven wrong, but proven wrong almost at the same time it is made. However, we believe there are a few things certain about the future of retail. They are:

That retail is bound to grow more complex as fractionalizing consumer demographics break into smaller and more lifestyle-specific segments.

That retail will become more competitive as a growing number of retailers strive to serve a narrower segment of increasingly sophisticated and indulged customers.

That the world loves international brands. And, a community loves its uniqueness.

Here, it is possible to posit another good bet for facing the future of retail; that the ability to shift business gears in the blink of a trend will remain an important survival tactic. Callison has grown into the world's number one provider of retail design in no small part because of its agility and speed in addressing change, and its ability to supply clients with quality tools to face that change as it does come.

**AYALA CENTER GREENBELT**
PLANNED AROUND THE CENTRAL PARK OF THE UPSCALE MAKATI DISTRICT OF CENTRAL MANILA, AYALA CENTER GREENBELT OPENED IN 2003 TO OVERWHELMING ACCOLADES BY RESIDENTS, TOURISTS, TENANTS AND COMMUNITY LEADERS. THE SITE WILL ACCOMMODATE FUTURE PHASES OF DEVELOPMENT, INCLUDING HOUSING, A HOTEL AND ADDITIONAL RETAIL AND ENTERTAINMENT.

## A Global Perspective

Whether global or local, the acceptance and recognition of the brand is critical to retail success. Branding carries with it the promise of relationship, a sort of pre-engagement agreement that will be fulfilled when the customer exchanges value, in this case, money, for identity, the chance to be associated with that brand. Having spent the last two decades designing for retail all over the world, Callison has developed an expertise in establishing brands and concepts that transcend specific cultures, or when appropriate, in ways that reflect and identify with those specific cultures.

This provides several important clues for the future of retail. One is that retail survivability in the future will depend on the ability of a business to convey the brand in a way the customer understands. Most importantly, communicating that branded message can take no longer than the time a shopper takes to walk past the store. In the future, the look, feel and touch of a store will be the devices through which the brand of a store is most efficiently communicated.

As a matter of course, Callison looks into areas that some still consider beyond the scope of, or incidental to, retail design. But the firm has found that looking at projects through the lenses of demography, sociology, branding, merchandising, graphic design and other "soft" fields, has become, in today's unforgiving retail environment, an essential part of successful design. Each of these disciplines has proven to be of tremendous strategic benefit for the realization of successful projects. In a sense, these new focal points are often what differentiate Callison design from plain architecture. In the future, it is likely that the field called "design" will grow ever less tolerant of miscues, and thus require the inclusion of areas of subject matter, seemingly even further removed from girders, bricks and window walls.

**SKYMART AT CHEK LAP KOK**
THE LARGEST SINGLE INTERNATIONAL AIRPORT RETAIL SPACE IN THE WORLD, SKYMART PRODUCES A SUBSTANTIAL PORTION OF HONG KONG AIRPORT'S OPERATING REVENUE. TO ENCOURAGE PEOPLE TO EXPLORE THE SHOPS AND RESTAURANTS, CALLISON INTRODUCED WARMER MATERIALS, COLORS AND SOFTER LIGHTING THAT DEFINE RETAIL "ZONES," WHILE STILL RELATING TO FOSTER PARTNERS' BOLD ARCHITECTURE OF THE TERMINAL DESIGN.

**NORDSTROM SPA**
REPRESENTING A CONVERGENCE OF THE FIRM'S RETAIL, HOSPITALITY AND HEALTHCARE EXPERIENCE, THE DESIGN FOR NORDSTROM SPAS ENVELOPS CUSTOMERS IN TRANQUIL, LUXURIOUS SURROUNDINGS.

**LA ENCANTADA**

A SPECIALTY SHOPPING CENTER IN THE HEART OF
TUCSON THAT IS INSPIRED BY ITS DISTINCTIVE
SOUTHWEST CULTURE, LA ENCANTADA IS DESIGNED
TO REFLECT THE ATTRIBUTES AND AMENITIES OF A
RESORT. DISTINCTIVE PLAZAS, NATIVE PLANTS AND
LANDSCAPING, AND MISSION-STYLE ARCHITECTURE
CREATE A RETAIL EXPERIENCE UNIQUE TO ITS
COMMUNITY AND CULTURE.

These days there are almost as many definitions of success in retail design as there are retail designers. Some believe all that is required is the design of a handsome edifice. Callison takes a totally different view. In the design world according to Callison, success boils down to a very simple proposition: retail success is a store, department store or shopping center that resonates with its customers to increase sales and traffic. As one Callison principal said about the need to balance design with business requirements; "great architecture is a given, it gets you in the door. At that point, it's how design overcomes the business challenges that will differentiate retail designers from their competitors."

## Meeting the Range of Retail Challenges

Over nearly three decades, Callison's formidable range of talented retail professionals has successfully met many and various of these business/design challenges. On a micro level, the firm has collaborated on store concepts and brand creation with leading retailers, developing the hundreds and even thousands of individual fixtures, displays and collateral required to make a store its own best advertisement.

At the macro level, Callison is responsible for designing or renovating some of the world's largest, most innovative and successful regional destination shopping centers.

**SOGO**

CALLISON WAS SELECTED BY SOGO
STORES OF JAPAN TO UPDATE ITS
IMAGE WITHOUT ALIENATING ITS
BROAD CUSTOMER BASE. ACHIEVED
BY INCORPORATING THE STORE'S
HISTORY INTO NEW DESIGN FOR THE
YOKOHAMA AND KOBE STORES, THE
PROJECT INCLUDED UPDATED VERSIONS
OF PUBLIC AREAS, NEW DEPARTMENT
CONCEPTS AND IMPROVED STORE
LAYOUTS.

Callison's across-the-board retail experience is unique in the design industry. It gives the firm the advantage of knowing — or of knowing how to find out — where a client's store concept will fit in the continuum of retail that is a shopping center or mall in the making. It also enables Callison to "fine tune" the mix of retail that goes into the center as well as the tenant planning that gives stores in similar affinity groups synergy by their physical proximity.

The future of retail will mean an end to the haphazard acceptance or placement of stores in a shopping center. Successful owners will have organized a very specific retail roster designed to match the needs and desires of the customers they want to attract and co-located merchandise in ways that draw in that particular demographic group.

In all three cases, success has a great deal to do with the character and cultural underpinnings that enable the right regional resonance to be sounded. Callison research strives to uncover as much detail as possible about the lives and aspirations of the project end users.

### Mixed-Use Destination Retail

If Callison's look ahead suggests anything, it is that mixed-use destinations will be one of the key drivers of the future of retail; places that will go beyond classifications such as "hotel," "resort," "conference center," "office building" or "shopping center."

Instead, there will be a place with names like "Grand Gateway," "Carillon Point," "Ayala Center," "Anaheim GardenWalk," places where people feel good about going because a range of their needs is met and because they feel at home and feel special. They will go there for a multitude of reasons — to see a movie, to eat, to use bike paths, to sit by a fountain, or to catch a train. And, of course, they will shop.

In Callison's estimation, the mixed-use destination is the future of retail because it is a place where people are not simply "consumers" consigned to stoking the engine of retail commerce. Instead, it will be a place where their needs as individuals are recognized and met in ways they identify with and want to return to again and again.

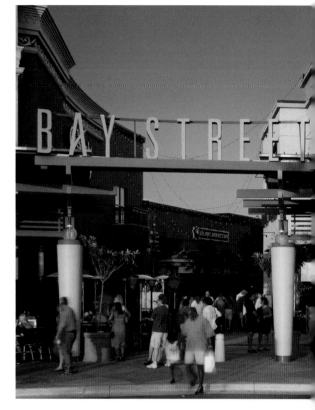

**BAY STREET AT INTERNATIONAL PLAZA**
THE DESIGN OF BAY STREET DERIVES ITS ENERGY FROM THE MULTICULTURAL HERITAGE OF THE TAMPA AREA. THE LIFESTYLE CENTER FEATURES UPSCALE RETAILERS, LOCAL BOUTIQUES, RESTAURANTS AND ENTERTAINMENT IN AN OPEN-AIR PEDESTRIAN-ORIENTED ATMOSPHERE.

# FLAT

## FLATIRON CROSSING

BROOMFIELD, COLORADO

The result of exceptional attention to local detail and astute retail thinking, FlatIron Crossing is a generational advance in mall design — a highly profitable and well-liked retail destination in tune with its environment and community.

Overlooking the prairie on Colorado Route 36 midway between Denver and Boulder, FlatIron Crossing is the Callison-designed regional destination shopping center that is the antidote to the generic malls that seemed to drop from outer space into communities around the world in the seventies and eighties.

### The Mall Redefined, Redesigned

In FlatIron Crossing, Callison has broken the mall open. The design focuses on the local lifestyle, which has a decided outdoors outlook, and pays tribute to the ragged, rugged mountains surrounding the Denver area that give it an undeniable appeal. The 1.5-million-square-foot FlatIron Crossing balances a two-level enclosed mall with an open-air village that is a mix of shops, restaurants and service providers finely tuned to the lifestyle and sensibility of the high-plains devotees who populate the Denver Basin.

The FlatIron experience begins with a meadowed slope on the southwestern side of the highway that draws the eye up to a complex of rustic outbuildings designed to reflect elements of rural design. These focus attention on two sinuous one-thousand-foot-long vaulted structures of glass, wood, steel and rusticated stone. At the right time of day, these buildings seem bathed in the same spectral hues as the nearby peaks. Similarly, the jutting angles of the roofline seem to mirror the jagged silhouette of the Flatiron Range. Using locally found and recycled materials for the project including stone from the Flatiron Range helped make the final product more environmentally friendly, more contextual and, remarkably, more affordable.

# IRON

FlatIron is designed to eliminate the prosaic "lets-take-in-the-whole-building-at-a-glance" straight-line design of older malls. Instead, the project's interior space moves in two sweeping arcs that naturally draw people between the indoor and outdoor features at the same time that it adds a "what's-around-the-corner?" curiosity factor.

What Callison has done at FlatIron is to bring the inside out and the outside in. This has, in effect, created the archetypal integrated indoor-outdoor regional shopping center. The result of Callison's highly focused attention to local detail is a highly profitable and successful retail center that is both respectful of its environment and in tune with its community.

From the opening of the mall in summer 2000 and the Village a year later, FlatIron was an immediate retail success with big crowds, sales per square foot double industry average, full occupancy and higher-than-target lease rates.

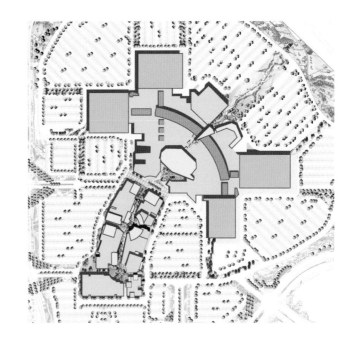

FlatIron Crossing elevates the purpose of a regional shopping center by realizing its potential as a legitimate venue for social, economic and cultural interaction.

NIKE

NIKE GODDESS

NEWPORT BEACH, CALIFORNIA

**In a bid to win more female consumers, the design for Nike's goddess stores highlights lifestyle over the footwear giant's traditional emphasis on performance. On the store's opening day, sales tripled projections and average purchases continue to beat the average purchase at the much larger Nike Towns.**

In 2000, Nike brought Callison on board to help capture the world's largest demographic — the female customer — it had to go through some serious soul searching. Through an innovative store concept and a new brand, called NIKEgoddess, the concept was to give women an appealing new way to view and buy Nike footwear, apparel and equipment. With its emphasis on a comfortable, modern environment with a residential appeal, the design represents a lifestyle approach rather than the sports imagery themes found in other Nike stores.

Recognizing the critical need to communicate a simple, powerful and unified brand message through every facet of the presentation, store design, merchandising and product design were developed simultaneously. The result is a study in how to reposition a predominantly masculine, sports-oriented brand image to tap into an active, fashion-conscious female customer base that has the power to significantly expand market share.

The design communicates the NIKEgoddess brand through choice of materials, colors, images, textures, lighting, scents and sounds, to create a harmonious relationship between product and environment that enabled the store to be its own best billboard.

## A Process Unfolds

To test the impact of every detail of design, a full-scale model of the store was built. Customers, focus groups, retailers and buyers were encouraged to physically experience the concept with design refinements made as the process unfolded.

Both Nike and Callison are accomplished practitioners in the art of research and, based on reviews of product information and competition and trends in the marketplace and desired personality attributes, a clear theme emerged: The women that NIKEgoddess wanted to attract were more comfortable shopping in a space that conveyed the feeling of home, rather than one of commerce. Thus, Callison based the architecture of the store on concepts of home and comfort by developing fixtures inspired by such home furnishings as credenzas and couches, providing an atmosphere of comfort modernism in which to showcase Nike's women's line.

Color palette is neutral, using dark and light woods mixed with pale blues to provide a rich and warm yet subtle backdrop for the product. Lighting throughout the store also reinforces the residential feel; the store is washed with lamps emitting a warm sunlight base color to bring out the true color of the product.

A runway in the center of the store, made of varying shades of blue mosaic glass tiles provides a distinct entry and product presentation focus while reinforcing the stores two distinctive halves — on one side a "boutique" which showcases products in a vignette style, using the display to tell the story about the product, while on the other side the "warehouse" provides density with a higher capacity fixture type.

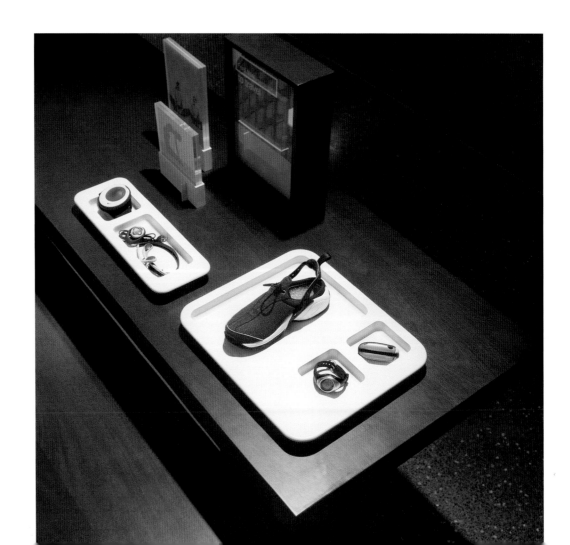

ALA MOANA CENTER

HONOLULU, HAWAII

With design that responds to a growing desire in Hawaii to preserve the islands' distinct culture, the expansion of Ala Moana enriches its ties to the community — to the tune of $1 billion in yearly sales.

### An Opportunity to Reposition

Retained initially to design a new upper level and fashion anchor for Honolulu's venerable Ala Moana Shopping Center, Callison was able to show owners, Daiei, Inc. and General Growth Management of Hawaii, that there would be increased patronage and higher revenue if the center was not only expanded, but also repositioned.

The immediate goal was to generate new excitement, a fresh retail identity and a closer connection to both the surrounding area and to the spirit of Hawaii. While the initial focus was on re-orienting Ala Moana, Callison was ultimately engaged to undertake not only architecture and interior design, but also research, environmental graphics and theming.

### New Connections, New Customers

Early research focused on potential new customers for the center, and quickly showed that the greatest source would be from the local community, not tourists. The solution Callison proposed was a physical and symbolic opening up and reconnection of the center to the surrounding land- and people-scape.

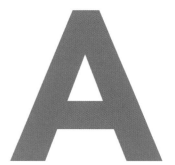

OANA

The symbolic reconnection with the community involved a design of the upper levels that aligned Ala Moana to the tropical environment of Hawaii. The means included opening up views to the beach and mountains, and the creation of a Pacific Islander village–style destination to replace the original food court. Working with Hawaiian authorities, Callison researched deeply into the use of local materials, plant life and symbolic island imagery.

## Much More than a Symbolic Success
Completed in 1999, the Ala Moana renovation is both a critical and business success. Critics praised the authenticity of a design that conveys a sense of the island's spirit without resorting to kitsch or cliché. And *Retail Traffic* described Ala Moana as "one of the most profitable shopping centers in the United States."

The business results speak for themselves. In the three years since the renovation, with an increase in leasable space from 1.5 to 1.8 million square feet, Ala Moana still produces sales exceeding $1000 per square foot and has taken in over one billion dollars per year in each of those years.

SCOTT

SCOTTSDALE FASHION SQUARE

SCOTTSDALE, ARIZONA

With a hospitality-driven persona that celebrates the desert resort lifestyle, the renovation and expansion of Scottsdale Fashion Square captured the attention of Scottsdale shoppers.

### Drawing a Bead on the End User

Prior to the design phase for the 450,000-square-foot expansion of the Scottsdale Fashion Square for Westcor Partners, Callison drew a research bead on what was the fastest growing segment of new Arizona residents. These were largely "empty nest" couples who had migrated from other parts of the U.S. to live in one of scores of "country club" developments springing up in the Phoenix/Scottsdale area.

This upper-income group translated into a pool of local shoppers whose loyalty to particular retail outlets, and a particular shopping center, represented a highly attractive target group.

### A Hospitality Solution

The solution for the Fashion Square expansion draws on the firm's hospitality knowledge, to re-create Scottsdale Fashion Square into a rich experience evocative of Scottsdale's grand resort hotels.

Customers arrive from a drive sweeping up to the porte cochere that forms a new formal entrance to Scottsdale Fashion Square. There they can alight, leaving their cars with valet parkers, before moving through a series of spacious, comfortable "lobbies," and a grand Rotunda "foyer," each area filled with beautiful, comfortable furnishings and luxuriant rugs.

The Scottsdale Fashion Square expansion opened in late 1998, its new hospitality-driven persona immediately capturing the imagination of Scottsdale shoppers. Opening quarter sales exceeded goals in new stores, while existing store sales jumped as much as 10%.

# SDALE

SOUT

SOUTH COAST PLAZA WEST

COSTA MESA, CALIFORNIA

With its contemporary re-imaging, South Coast Plaza West is a premier example of transforming vacated anchor space into a collection of the top names in lifestyle retailing.

Callison designed the renovation of South Coast Plaza West, formerly named Crystal Court, to become the lifestyle extension of the main shopping center of South Coast Plaza.

To attract new tenants like Crate & Barrel, Borders and other lifestyle-oriented retailers, the conversion went deeper than surface cosmetics to recreate a simple, yet elegant architecture on an urban scale — a design approach that complemented the prevalent contemporary architecture of South Coast Plaza's office and retail core developed by Henry Segerstrom. A pre-existing Robinson's-May store was successfully converted to accentuate the presence of multiple mini majors on the building exterior and activate the three interior levels. A three-story feature window further opens up retail interior, which also supports a pedestrian bridge that connects South Coast Plaza West to the main South Coast Plaza.

The repositioned South Coast Plaza West, integrated as it is with South Coast Plaza, has become the success that its owners envisioned, as demonstrated by an occupancy rate that has doubled and sales that have met or exceeded expectations since the project reopened.

JORD

JORDAN CREEK TOWN CENTER

WEST DES MOINES, IOWA

Advancing the concept of the regional shopping center as both destination and community heart, Callison's plan for Jordan Creek Town Center builds on momentum from the commercial and design successes of FlatIron Crossing and Ayala Center Greenbelt.

Taking the theme of integration with both the natural environment and the community, the Jordan Creek plan envisions a two-level retail galleria blended with two spectacular outdoor public spaces. The first is the "Village District," a 750,000-square-foot community center with open-air shopping featuring national retailers and specialty shops and restaurants. The other, the "Lake District," is the entertainment zone, with clubs, restaurants, shops and a 150-room hotel built on the shores of a three-acre lake created at the site. More than scenery or its water feature, the Lake District will provide the kinds of "boardwalk" activities that make going to the lake or the beach such appealing destinations.

Inspired by the country club lifestyle, the center's design uses textures and hues to reflect a casual and understated elegance. Incorporating four anchor stores and approximately 375,000 square feet of leasable area, the two-story mall forms a gentle arc with an upper-level retail and entertainment component incorporating a 1,000-seat food court, a 22-screen Cineplex and a "Market" spine opening up to the lake front.

Enhancing its potential to be a landmark destination in the greater Des Moines area, Jordan Creek pays special attention to the landscaping, hardscape and waterscaping within the 200-acre site, incorporating bicycle paths, trails, promenades and several picturesque waterfalls.

# SPA

## SPACE NEEDLE PAVILION

SEATTLE, WASHINGTON

A new, base-level public plaza, store and dramatic entryway to Seattle's iconic Space Needle enriches the visitor experience of the unmistakable 605-foot tower, and maintains its viability as an attraction.

In 2000, Callison undertook an exceptional assignment, for which was crafted a solution that drew inspiration from Callison's retail, hospitality and mixed-use practices. The project was the refurbishment of the Seattle Space Needle, the Northwest's most famous man-made landmark.

### Befitting, But Not Overshadowing

Completed in 1962, in time for the Seattle "Century 21" World's Fair, the Needle's entrance had been a hastily improvised portal that for nearly forty years had kept visitors standing in an uninspiring queue. The entry was considered a serious weak point in the Space Needle experience and Callison's task was to design both a "back door" connection with the Seattle Center to the south and a new "front door" entryway to downtown that befitted a major attraction, and yet did not overshadow or clash with the landmark structure.

### Ramping Up

The most significant change is the ground-level addition of a 40-foot-tall glass-enclosed pavilion that replaced the existing retail, ticketing and lobby facilities. Resembling a transparent nautilus encircling the three-legged base of the Space Needle, the addition is made up of two components: A 360° circulation ramp that winds around the legs of the Space Needle, and a sloping cylindrical building nestled inside the base, which houses the new retailing as well as the elevator entrances. The whole structure touches the Space Needle as lightly as possible, both physically and visually.

People going up to the observation deck will enter at ground level and, as they wind up the ramp, they encounter tantalizing views of the retail below, the 4,000-square-foot store called SpaceBase. After enjoying the view from the top, they descend in one of the three elevators that deposits them finally into the retail portion.

C E N E

Nothing is square in the transparent pavilion building and no columns obstruct the view. The building is cone-shaped and slopes inward at 83.5 degrees. The spiral ramp cantilevers outside the legs of the Needle, continually tapering as it wraps the cone with the outside curtain wall, leaning out at 96.5 degrees.

## A New Approach

To create a grander entry, Callison began with the approach to the Space Needle, designing two new public plazas with sweeping motor-vehicle drives that emulated the "flying saucer" shape of the Needle's top and could be closed off for special events. The south plaza linked up with the Seattle Center, the landscaped 74-acre campus that is the fourth largest visitor destination in the United States and home to Seattle's leading cultural and educational organizations, sports teams, theater groups, museums and other entertainment venues including the Callison-designed Boeing IMAX Theater and Ackerley Family Gallery and Seattle Repertory Theater.

For the downtown-facing entryway, Callison also created a more visible and memorable "front door" to the Space Needle, expanding and enhancing the North Plaza with a new fountain, landscaping and seating, and completing this down-town-facing entryway was a grand porte cochere.

# HARR

## HARRODS WHITE HALL

LONDON, ENGLAND

With its reinvented White Hall cosmetics department, Harrods maintains its distinction as an icon of beauty and grandeur while responding to changing trends in cosmetics retailing.

Harrods Knightsbridge collaborated with Callison to transform the White Hall, home of the world's most celebrated beauty brands, with a luminous new look and a powerful new approach to cosmetic retailing. The result is today's state-of-the-art model for the modern beauty department, with all of Harrods familiar substance and style.

### Removing Barriers to Beauty

Cosmetics sales and service at the high-end of the market has moved far more toward a customer/advisor sales method, with beauty advisors actively engaging their clients to interact with a brand's makeup stations and displays. As a result, the re-created White Hall did away with an across-the-counter style of service in favor of interactive techniques and heightened service levels akin to the individual attention of a salon or boutique shop. In the spirit of inspiration and discovery, there are more spaces inviting customers to experience products through touch, smell and sampling.

O D S

With its stunning palette of white marble, glass and stone, the White Hall's uncluttered, boutique-like setting supplies the perfect backdrop to the Harrod's beauty experience. Lighting in the hall was also enhanced for a more accurate portrayal of color, from dark and indirect to a lighting that is bright and warm with a glow at customer level ideal for trying on beauty products.

With numerous strategies to remove barriers and promote discovery, to showcase the brands and illuminate the space, Harrods White Cosmetics Hall has reached a new level of distinction, creating a warm and personalized experience that is true to Harrods' unsurpassed customer service.

# DEIR

## DEIRA CITY CENTRE

DUBAI, UNITED ARAB EMIRATES

With its third expansion, Deira City Centre continues to be one of Dubai's most viable and most visited retail/ entertainment destinations.

Historically, the merchant-sheiks of the kingdoms that today make up the United Arab Emirates were recognized for their trading skills. This was particularly true of Dubai, a fishing village that by the beginning of the twentieth century was said to have the largest souks on the Gulf Coast, with 350 shops in the Deira district alone. Merchants came from India and Iran, drawn by the potential for profit in the great markets of Dubai, the acknowledged trading center of the region.

At the start of another century, Dubai has maintained its standing as the center of regional trade. To maintain that advantage into the future, the government of Dubai has encouraged developers to expand the trading geography beyond the region and make Dubai a hub between East and West.

In 1993, Callison was hired by Majid Al Futtaim Investments, LLC, to do the master planning, architecture, interior design, and graphic design for a new, 845,000-square-foot mixed-use retail and entertainment center for Deira City, once and still the commercial center of Dubai. The Deira City Centre was designed to do on a smaller scale what Dubai had done on a larger one; profit from integrating the commerce of two distinct worlds.

A C I

In the case of the Deira City Centre, such international anchor tenants as the Continent hypermarket and Ikea are comfortably ensconced with more regional retailers with a tradition of the souk. The design also draws on different cultures; it is defined by dramatic tent structures that reference traditional Bedouin forms, the courts provide natural lighting for the interior and create a strong signature for the shopping center.

Since its opening in 1995, Deira City Centre has become Dubai's most visited retail/ entertainment destination, and truly a place that meets the needs of both the local and tourist populations, in a way that is economically, socially and culturally relevant.

SEIB
SEIBU DEPARTMENT STORE

MULTIPLE LOCATIONS, JAPAN

As an integral part of their long-term renovation and expansion plan, Callison has helped define and implement new retail strategies that develop Seibu's image as a fashion leader.

### Embracing Change

Seibu became Asia's leading department store chain and a recognized trendsetter because, since its beginning in 1940, the store has embraced change rather than fought it. In 1995, Seibu hired Callison not only for help modernizing its stores but, perhaps most importantly, to help define and implement new retail strategies in response to the changing attitudes and lifestyles sweeping Japan and beyond.

Callison began its collaboration with Seibu by undertaking the renovation of the flagship store at Ikebukuro. The goal was to improve the customer's shopping experience through more efficient planning, more dramatic display and lighting and heightened levels of customer comfort. The success at Ikebukuro led to similar work by Callison at Seibu stores in Gobankan, Shizuoka and Funabashi and Shibuya.

Success led to a contract to design and implement a program enabling Seibu to improve sales and heighten its image as a fashion leader. The mechanism for change would be a chain-wide commitment to a new level of customer service. Callison's response was to design a program to define and focus Seibu's brand and apply it across 60 departments.

U D E P

**Horizons Beyond Design**

Callison's program included work sessions, focus groups and training. The first step was to identify key Seibu values as well as the target customer, then address both in every aspect of the company, including areas such as human resources, customer service, merchandise mix, store planning and store design. Callison's Visual Merchandising team was called in to hold a yearlong series of staff-training sessions. The team also created the Seibu Visual Merchandising Standards Manual, a resource guide now used throughout the 35-store chain.

The result was impressive. In the first month following the completion of the program, Seibu rang up a 14.5% increase in sales per square foot, while setting a new benchmark for retail service in Asia.

At the same time, Seibu was also interested in learning about shopping centers as an alternative retailing format, and asked Callison to help them become the first Japanese company to build and operate a portfolio of suburban shopping centers. With Callison's involvement, Seibu created the Millennium Development Company. Its first shopping center, the Aurora Mall opened in 2000 in Higashi Totsuka, after a Callison-led education and networking effort that included an international shopping center tour, introductions to international developers and lenders, advice on ownership and lease structures, the requirements of international retailers and shopping center management.

# GLOBAL OPPORTUNITIES
## Producing Sparks with New Urban Ideas

Some of the liveliest expressions of urban destinations appear in Callison's next chapter. These destinations are in places where societal, demographic and economic situations demand the "smarter place" principles that not only create exciting projects, but also ones that prove to be business successes. We are experiencing the excitement of cities, urban districts and regions that are driven to accelerate their development, driving us to take the multi-use urban destination to a new level.

As much of our work in progress illustrates, embracing the global also means embracing the energy of mixed-use. Whether creating new, remaking old or building connections between them, the urban ideal is found in the sustainability of multiple uses in one location. As we apply and expand our expertise on these exciting opportunities, it sparks new design thinking that impacts the work we are doing everywhere.

AL NAKHEEL
DUBAI, UAE

**EMIRATES EXPERIENCE**
DUBAI, UAE

**DMCC TOWER**
DUBAI, UAE

## NAWRAS VILLAS
DUBAI, UAE

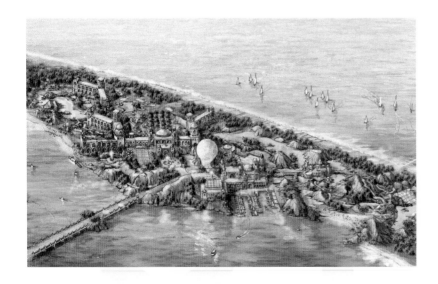

## AQUATICA
DUBAI, UAE

## THE CREEK LANDING
DUBAI, UAE

## CONTINENT CENTRE
ABU DHABI, UAE

## THE GARDENS
DUBAI, UAE

## EARTH ISLE
DUBAI, UAE

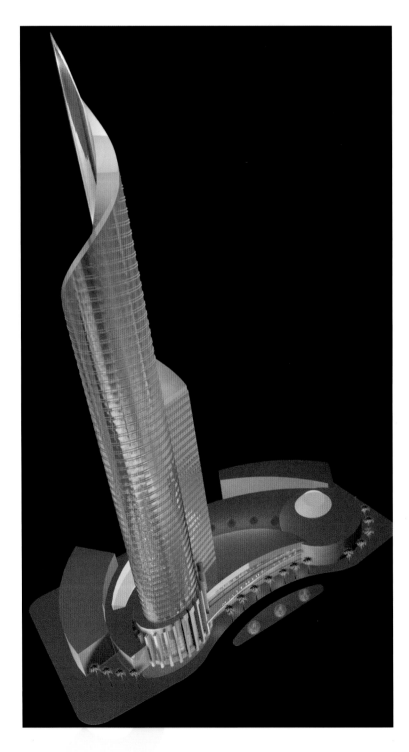

## PEARL OF THE GULF
### DOHA, QATAR

## ALSHAYA OFFICE TOWER
### KUWAIT CITY, KUWAIT

## AYALA NORTH TRIANGLE
MANILA, PHILLIPINES

## GURO CENTER
SEOUL, KOREA

## LG MART
SEOUL, KOREA

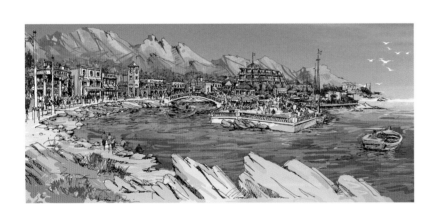

## AIJIAN SHOPPING CENTER
HARBIN, CHINA

## QINGDAO SHILAOREAN TOURISM RESORT
QINGDAO, CHINA

## CENTRAL AVENUE
CHONGQING, CHINA

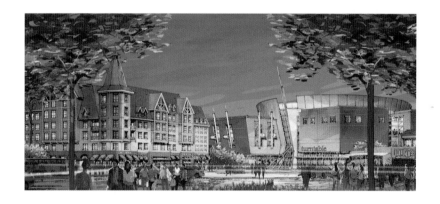

## NANJING ROAD
SHANGHAI, CHINA

## XINGHAI BAY
DALIAN, CHINA

## XIAOSHAN MIXED-USE
### XIAOSHAN, CHINA

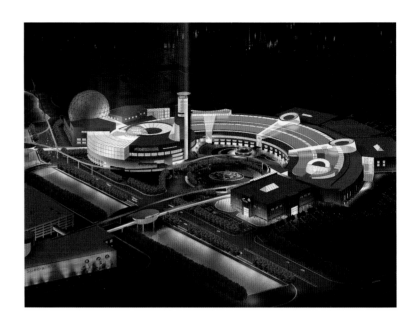

## NEW CENTURY SQUARE
### SONGJIANG, CHINA

## ZHONG GUAN CUN
### BEIJING, CHINA

## NO. 1 DEPARTMENT STORE
SHANGHAI, CHINA

## IKEA
MULTIPLE LOCATIONS, RUSSIA

# SELECTED CHRONOLOGY

1973
NORDSTROM
SPOKANE, WA

1975
PARK PLACE BUILDING
SEATTLE, WA

1976
HILTON HOTEL
SEATTLE, WA

NORDSTROM
PORTLAND, OR

NORDSTROM VANCOUVER MALL
VANCOUVER, WA

1977
NORDSTROM
YAKIMA, WA

1978
NORDSTROM SOUTH
COAST PLAZA
COSTA MESA, CA

1979
NORTHWEST MANAGEMENT
EASTLAKE BUILDING
SEATTLE, WA

NORDSTROM BREA MALL
BREA, CA

NORDSTROM NORTHGATE MALL
SEATTLE, WA

1980
CROWNE PLAZA MALL
SEATTLE, WA

EVERGREEN GENERAL HOSPITAL
SEATTLE, WA

MADISON HOTEL
SEATTLE, WA

WESTMONT HOTEL
FISHERMAN'S WHARF
SAN FRANCISCO, CA

1981
NORDSTROM BELLEVUE SQUARE
BELLEVUE, WA

NORDSTROM LOS CERRITOS
CERRITOS, CA

SEATAC MARRIOT AIRPORT
SEATAC, WA

RAMADA HOTEL
BOTHELL, WA

1982
BARANOF HOTEL
JUNEAU, AK

KOLL CENTER
BELLEVUE, WA

PUGET SOUND HOSPITAL
TACOMA, WA

1983
HONOLULU INTERNATIONAL
AIRPORT RETAIL
HONOLULU, HI

NORDSTROM GLENDALE
GALLERIA
GLENDALE, CA

1984
FASHION BAR
MULTIPLE LOCATIONS, COLORADO

IBM OFFICES
SEATTLE, WA

MICROSOFT PHASE I
REDMOND, WA

NORDSTROM STANFORD
CENTER
PALO ALTO, CA

NORDSTROM TOPANGA PLAZA
CANOGA PARK, CA

PROVIDENCE HOSPITAL
EVERETT, WA

1985
NORDSTROM HORTON PLAZA
SAN DIEGO, CA

THE INN AT SEMIAHMOO
BLAINE, WA

GTE NORTHWEST
HEADQUARTERS
EVERETT, WA

1986
BLUE CROSS CAMPUS
MOUNTLAKE TERRAS, WA

MICROSOFT PHASE II
REDMOND, WA

VIRGINIA MASON HOSPITAL
FEDERAL WAY, WA

1987
CARILLON POINT
KIRKLAND, WA

LANE POWELL
MULTIPLE LOCATIONS

NORDSTROM MAIN PLACE
SANTA ANA, CA

TANJONG PAGAR
SINGAPORE

1988
CITY CENTRE
SEATTLE, WA

NORDSTROM SAN FRANCISCO
CENTRE
SAN FRANCISCO, CA

NORDSTROM TYSONS CORNER
MCLEAN, VA

1989
HARBOR STEPS
SEATTLE, WA

NORSTROM FASHION CENTER
AT PENTAGON CITY
ARLINGTON, VA

RAFFLES HOTEL RETAIL
SINGAPORE

ROGUE VALLEY
MEDICAL CENTER
MEDFORD, OR

**1990**

BOEING CUSTOMER SERVICE
TRAINING CENTER
RENTON, WA

KULA BAY STORES
MULTIPLE LOCATIONS

NORDSTROM PASEO NUEVO MALL
SANTA BARBARA, CA

SPACE NEEDLE RESTAURANT
SEATTLE, WA

**1991**

ARGENT HOTEL
SAN FRANCISCO, CA

NORDSTROM OAKBROOK CENTER
OAKBROOK, IL

PACIFIC SCIENCE CENTER
PLANETARIUM
SEATTLE, WA

PROVIDENCE ALASKA
MEDICAL CENTER
ANCHORAGE, AK

SEATTLE HEIGHTS
SEATTLE, WA

WASHINGTON STATE
UNIVERSITY ENGINEERING
TEACHING & RESEARCH
BUILDING
PULLMAN, WA

**1992**

BELLEVUE ATHLETIC CLUB
HOTEL
BELLEVUE, WA

FASHION SHOW MALL
LAS VEGAS, NV

MICROSOFT BUILDING 25
REDMOND, WA

NORDSTROM MALL OF AMERICA
BLOOMINGTON, MN

PROVIDENCE
HEALTHCARE CENTER
MURPHY'S CORNER, WA

SEATTLE CENTER CENTERHOUSE
SEATTLE, WA

ST. CHARLES MEDICAL CENTER
BEND, OR

TAISHO LIFE INSURANCE
CORPORATE HEADQUARTERS
TOKYO, JAPAN

WHITE PINE LODGE
SANDPOINT, ID

**1993**

ACT THEATRE
SEATTLE, WA

CITY CENTER TOWER
BELLEVUE, WA

GRAND GATEWAY
SHANGHAI, CHINA

OTA SHOPPING CENTER
OTA, JAPAN

SCOTTSDALE FASHION SQUARE
SCOTTSDALE, AZ

**1994**

BANK OF CHINA
SHANGHAI, CHINA

EDDIE BAUER HEADQUARTERS
REDMOND, WA

MICROSOFT BUILDINGS 26, 27
REDMOND, WA

SEATTLE REPERTORY THEATER
SEATTLE, WA

**1995**

AYALA GREENBELT MASTER
PLAN
MANILA, PHILIPPINES

BIG MOUNTAIN SKI RESORT
WHITEFISH, MT

BOEING IMAX
THEATER/ACKERLEY FAMILY
EXHIBIT GALLERY
SEATTLE, WA

FUTURE@WORK I
SEATTLE, WA

HEWLETT PACKARD
ROHNERT PARK, CA

KCPQ BROADCAST STUDIO
SEATTLE, WA

LAKEPOINTE MIXED-USE
DEVELOPMENT
KENMORE, WA

L.L. BEAN
MACLEAN, VA

MA ON SHAN RESIDENTIAL
COMPLEX
HONG KONG

MICROSOFT TROON
REDMOND, WA

SKYMART AT CHEK LAP KOK
HONG KONG

**1996**

DEIRA CITY CENTER
DUBAI, U.A.E.

NORDSTROM PARK MEADOWS
DENVER, CO

RANGSIT PLAZA
BANGKOK, THAILAND

W HOTEL SEATTLE
SEATTLE, WA

WELLPOINT HEALTH NETWORKS
EXECUTIVE CENTER
THOUSAND OAKS, CA

**1997**

1700 SEVENTH
SEATTLE, WA

AYALA CENTER GREENBELT 3
MANILA, PHILIPPINES

BELLEVUE COMMUNITY
COLLEGE STUDENT UNION
BELLEVUE, WA

FLATIRON CROSSING
BROOMFIELD, CO

HEWLETT PACKARD
FORT COLLINS, CO

KEY CENTER
BELLEVUE, WA

LATHAM & WATKINS
ORANGE COUNTY
ORANGE COUNTY, CA

ONE CONVENTION PLACE
SEATTLE, WA

PROVIDENCE SEATTLE MEDICAL
CENTER
SEATTLE, WA

WELLS FARGO/STARBUCKS
MULTIPLE LOCATIONS

WESTIN HOTEL
WESTMINSTER, CO

**1998**

BAYSTREET AT INTERNATIONAL
PLAZA
TAMPA, FL

COOLEY GODWARD LLP
BELLEVUE, WA

HQ EXECUTIVE SUITES
MULTIPLE LOCATIONS

METROPOLITAN TOWER
SEATTLE, WA

NORDSTROM DOWNTOWN
SEATTLE
SEATTLE, WA

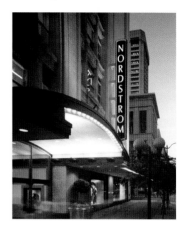

RIVER PARK SQUARE
SPOKANE, WA

SEIBU DEPARTMENT STORE
IKEBURO, JAPAN

SOUTH COAST PLAZA WEST
COSTA MESA, CA

TETON CLUB
JACKSON HOLE, WY

**1999**

ACKERLEY GROUP BUILDING
SEATTLE, WA

ALA MOANA CENTER
HONOLULU, HI

AYALA STATION
MANILA, PHILIPPINES

BEVERLY CENTER
LOS ANGELES, CA

DELTA LODGE
WHISTLER, BRITISH COLUMBIA

GAP FLAGSHIP STORES
MULTIPLE LOCATIONS

GIANTS BUILDING
SAN FRANCISCO, CA

ORRICK, HERRINGTON &
SUTCLIFFE, LLP
MENLO PARK, CA

SEIBU DEPARTMENT STORE
MULTIPLE LOCATIONS, JAPAN

ST. CHARLES CENTER FOR
HEALTH & LEARNING
BEND, OR

ST. JOSEPH'S HOSPITAL
TACOMA, WA

**2000**

AEKYUNG DEPARTMENT STORE
SEOUL, KOREA

AGILENT TECHNOLOGIES
ROHNERT PARK, CA

ANAHEIM GARDENWALK
SAN DIEGO, CA

FUTURE@WORK II
SEATTLE, WA

GOLDMAN SACHS
SEATTLE, WA

LA ENCANTADA
TUCSON, AZ

NIKEGODDESS
NEWPORT BEACH, CA

NORDSTROM MICHIGAN AVENUE
CHICAGO, IL

NORTHPARK SHOPPING CENTER
DALLAS, TX

ORRICK, HERRINGTON &
SUTCLIFFE, LLP
SEATTLE, WA

WAVVE COMMUNICATIONS
SACRAMENTO, CA

**2001**

BOEING WORLD
HEADQUARTERS
CHICAGO, IL

CINGULAR WIRELESS
MULTIPLE LOCATIONS

DFS GALLERIA
SINGAPORE

HARRODS WHITE HALL
LONDON, ENGLAND

NORDSTROM EASTON TOWN
CENTER
COLUMBUS, OH

POTTERY BARN
MULTIPLE LOCATIONS

SEIBU DEPARTMENT STORE
SHIBUYA, JAPAN

SOGO
MULTIPLE LOCATIONS, JAPAN

SUWON GATEWAY PLAZA
SEOUL, KOREA

WILLIAMS SONOMA
MULTIPLE LOCATIONS

WOLA PARK SHOPPING CENTER
WARSAW, POLAND

**2002**

COLDWATER CREEK
MULTIPLE LOCATIONS

IKEA DEVELOPMENTS
RUSSIA

LATHAM & WATKINS
FRANKFURT, GERMANY

LG DEPARTMENT STORE
BUCHEON, KOREA

MEYDENBAUER
BELLEVUE, WA

NORDSTROM LAS VEGAS
LAS VEGAS, NV

NORDSTROM THE GROVE AT
FARMERS MARKET
LOS ANGELES, CA

SONGJIANG MIXED-USE
COMPLEX
SONGJIANG, SHANGHAI, CHINA

THE VILLAGE AT MAMMOTH
MAMMOTH LAKES, CA

WANGFUJING DEPARTMENT
STORE
BEIJING, CHINA

WASHINGTON MUTUAL
EXECUTIVE OFFICES
SEATTLE, WA

WASHINGTON MUTUAL IRVINE
CAMPUS
IRVINE, CA

**2003**

COASTALCADE MIXED-USE
RESORT
XINGHAI BAY, CHINA

KUSI MIXED-USE
SAN DIEGO, CA

NANJING ROAD
SHANGHAI, CHINA

NORDSTROM ALDERWOOD
MALL
LYNWOOD, WA

RIO DE JUMERIAH
DUBAI, U.A.E.

VILLAGE AT SOUTHLANDS
DENVER, CO

# AWARDS

## 2003

**Finalist, ULI Award for Excellence**
Ayala Center Greenbelt
Manila, Philippines

**Outstanding Merit**
**NASFM Retail Design Awards**
Nordstrom
Las Vegas, Nevada

**Certificate of Merit, ICSC International Design & Development Awards**
Bay Street
Tampa, Florida

**Citation, Modern Healthcare Design Awards**
St. Charles Center for Health and Learning
Bend, Oregon

## 2002

**Honor Award**
**Oregon Chapter, International Interior Design Association**
Nike Goddess
Newport Beach, California

**Technology Building of the Year**
**National Association of Industrial & Office Parks**
Microsoft Building 50
Redmond, Washington

**GRAND SADI, Shopping Center World**
NikeGoddess
Newport Beach, California

**Outstanding Merit, Softline Specialty Store, NASFM Awards**
NikeGoddess
Newport Beach, California

**Gold Award, Resort Architecture, American Resort Development Association Awards**
The Delta Whistler Resort
Whistler, B.C., Canada

**Design Award, ICSC International Design & Development Awards**
FlatIron Crossing
Broomfield, Colorado

**First Place, New Centers**
**Shopping Center World SADI Award**
FlatIron Crossing
Broomfield, Colorado

**First Place, New Stores**
**Shopping Center World SADI Award**
Nike Goddess

**First Place, Renovated Centers**
**Shopping Center World SADI Award**
Beverly Center
Los Angeles, California

**Honorable Mention, New Stores**
**Shopping Center World SADI Award**
Cingular Wireless Prototype

## 2001

**First Place, Hard Lines Under 5,000 SF, Chain Store Age Retail Store of the Year**
Cingular Wireless Prototype Store
Multiple Locations

**First Place, Shopping Center**
**Chain Store Age Retail Store of the Year**
FlatIron Crossing
Broomfield, Colorado

**Honorable Mention, Store within a Store, Chain Store Age Retail Store of the Year**
Seibu Women's Designer Shoe Department
Shibuya, Tokyo, Japan

**Honorable Mention, VM+SD International Store Design Competition**
Cingular Wireless Prototype Stores
Multiple locations

**Honorable Mention, VM+SD International Store Design Competition**
Seibu Women's Designer Shoe Department
Shibuya, Tokyo, Japan

**Northwest Design Awards, Washington State Chapter American Society of Interior Designers**
Ackerley Communications Group Headquarters
Seattle, Washington

**Award for Excellence: Large-scale, Residential, Urban Land Institute**
Harbor Steps
Seattle, Washington

**Golden Token Award--Best New Facility, International Association for the Leisure & Entertainment Industry**
Illusionz
Issaquah, Washington

**Gold Award, Resort Architecture, American Resort Development Association**
Teton Club
Jackson Hole, Wyoming

**Design Award, ICSC International Design and Development Awards**
Ala Moana Shopping Center
Honolulu, Hawaii

**Certificate of Merit, ICSC International Design and Development Awards**
River Park Square
Spokane, Washington

**First Place, Shopping Center World SADI Award**
FlatIron Crossing
Broomfield, Colorado

**First Place, Shopping Center World SADI Award**
Seibu Department Store
Okazaki, Japan

## 2000

**Architectural Design Award of Excellence**
**Northwest Construction's Best of 2000**
Space Needle Expansion
Seattle, Washington

**Private Project Award of Excellence**
**Northwest Construction's Best of 2000**
Space Needle Expansion
Seattle, Washington

**First Place, VM+SD International Store Design Competition**
Illusionz
Issaquah, Washington

**Honorable Mention, VM+SD International Store Design Competition**
Halogen In-store Shop
Multiple locations

**Honorable Mention, VM+SD International Store Design Competition**
Nordstrom
Chicago, Illinois

**Honorable Mention, VM+SD International Store Design Competition**
FlatIron Crossing Food Court
Broomfield, Colorado

**First Place, International Over 100,000 SF Chain Store Age Retail Store of the Year**
Seibu
Higashi Totsuka, Yokohama-shi Kanagawa, Japan

**First Place, Shop within a Store**
**Chain Store Age Retail Store of the Year**
Nordstrom Halogen
Mall of Georgia

**First Place, Shopping Center**
**Chain Store Age Retail Store of the Year**
FlatIron Crossing
Broomfield, Colorado

**Award of Merit, American Institute of Architects, Pacific Northwest chapter**
KCPQ Broadcast Studio
Seattle, Washington

**Design Award**
**American Graphic Design Awards**
Illusionz
Issaquah, Washington

**Design Award**
**ICSC International Design and Development Awards**
Scottsdale Fashion Square
Scottsdale, Arizona

**Honorable Mention, Shopping Center World SADI Award**
Ala Moana Center
Honolulu, Hawaii

## 1999

**Superior Design Award, City of Redmond Architectural Design Awards**
Eddie Bauer Headquarters
Redmond, Washington

First Place, Shopping Center
World SADI Award
Seibu Department Store
Funabashi, Japan                                    1997

First Place, Shopping Center
World SADI Award
Scottsdale Fashion Square
Scottsdale, Arizona

First Place, Excellence in Masonry Design,
Washington Masonry Institute
River Park Square
Spokane, Washington

First Place, Chain Store Age Retail Store
of the Year, Shopping Center Category
Scottsdale Fashion Square
Scottsdale, Arizona

Honorable Mention, VM+SD International
Store Design Competition
Seibu Department Store
Higashi Totsuka, Japan

Honorable Mention, VM+SD International    1996
Store Design Competition
Ala Moana Center Food Court
Honolulu, Hawaii

1998

Honor Award, American Institute of
Architects, Seattle chapter
KCPQ Broadcast Studio
Seattle, Washington

Honor Award, American Institute of
Architects, Pacific Northwest chapter
A Contemporary Theatre (ACT)              1995
Seattle, Washington

Honor Award, Vista Design Awards
St. Charles Medical Center - Phase 6
Bend, Oregon

Honor Award, Washington Masonry Institute
Washington State University Engineering
Teaching Research Laboratory
Pullman, Washington

1994

First Place, VM+SD International Store
Design Competition
Trish McEvoy In-store Concept
Various locations

First Place, VM+SD International Store
Design Competition
Pacific Science Center Signage
Seattle, Washington

Honorable Mention, VM+SD International
Store Design Competition
Nordstrom
Seattle, Washington

Honorable Mention, VM+SD International    1993
Store Design Competition
Wells Fargo/Starbucks Prototype
Various locations

Buildings Magazine Modernization Award
Nordstrom
Seattle, Washington

Award of Merit, American Institute of
Architects, Seattle chapter
A Contemporary Theatre (ACT)
Seattle, Washington

Regional Winner for Urban Revitalization,
Urban Land Institute                       1992
ACT Theater
Seattle, Washington

Certificate of Merit, ICSC International
Design and Development Awards,
Innovative Design and New Construction
Deira City Centre
Dubai, United Arab Emirates

Certificate of Merit, ICSC International
Design and Development Awards,
Existing Renovation or Expansion
Fashion Show Mall
Las Vegas, Nevada

Certificate of Merit, ICSC International
Design and Development Awards,
Existing Renovation or Expansion
Laguna Hills Shopping Center
Laguna Hills, California

Certificate of Merit, ICSC International
Design and Development Awards,
Existing Renovation or Expansion
St. Clair Square
Fairview Heights, Illinois

1991

Northwest PMI Award
Boeing Customer Services Training Center
Seattle, Washington

Certificate of Merit, ICSC International    1990
Design and Development Awards,
Renovation or Expansion of an Existing
Center
Metrocenter
Phoenix, Arizona

Certificate of Merit, ICSC International
Design and Development Awards,
Existing Renovation or Expansion
Park Royal Shopping Center
Vancouver, British Columbia, Canada

Certificate of Merit, ICSC International
Design and Development Awards,         1989
Existing Renovation or Expansion
Topanga Plaza
Los Angeles, California

Urban Development Institute Award (Canada)
Park Royal Shopping Center
Vancouver, British Columbia, Canada

Excellence in Construction, American    1988
Subcontractors Association, Single Project
Award Over Seven Million
Metrocenter Mall
Phoenix, Arizona

Honorable Mention Monitor Magazine,
Stores of Excellence
Nordstrom
Mall of America, Bloomington, Minnesota

Certificate of Merit, ICSC International
Design and Development Awards,
Existing Renovation or Expansion
The Galleria at Tyler
Riverside, California

Honor Award, American Institute of
Architects (AIA) Northwest and Pacific
Region Conference Design Awards Program
The Inn at Semiahmoo
Blaine, Washington

Award of Merit, National Association of
Store Fixture Manufactures (NASFM)
Kula Bay
Multiple locations, California, Florida, Hawaii

Office Building of the Year, Building
Owners and Managers Association (BOMA)
Pacific First Centre (now City Centre)
Seattle, Washington

Honorable Mention, Monitor Magazine,
Stores of Excellence
Nordstrom
Paseo Nuevo, Santa Barbara, California

Certificate of Merit, ICSC International
Design and Development Awards,
Existing Renovation or Expansion
Westroads
Omaha, Nebraska

Design Excellence Awards, American
Society of Interior Designers (ASID), Seattle
Kula Bay
Multiple locations in Hawaii, California and Florida

First Place, National Association of Industrial
and Office Parks, Mixed-Use
Carillon Point
Kirkland, Washington

Honorable Mention, American Society of
Interior Designers (ASID)
Tilt at the Island
San Mateo, California

Office Development of the Year, SIOR
Boeing Employee's Credit Union
Washington

Honor Awards, American Institute of
Architects, Seattle
The Inn at Semiahmoo
Blaine, Washington

Store of Excellence, Monitor Magazine
Nordstrom at Tyson Corners
McLean, Virginia

First Place, National Association of Industrial
and Office Parks, Office Build-to-Suit
Microsoft World Headquarters
Redmond, Washington

# IMAGE CREDITS

**FOREWORD**

All photographs by Chris Eden

**ESSAYS**

Living Locally Competing Globally
All photographs by Chris Eden
p.10, Oyala rendering by Callison

Creating Smarter Places
All photographs by Chris Eden except
p. 36, Carillon Point

Hospitality as an Attitude
All photographs by Chris Eden except
p. 81, Harbor Steps, Fred Licht
p. 81, Bellevue Athletic Club, JF Housel
p. 83, Providence Health System, Steve Keating

Putting the Office to Work
All photographs by Chris Eden except
p. 143, KCPQ, Patrick Barta

Special Delivery
All photographs by Chris Eden except
p. 178, WAVVE, Ed Asmus
p. 179, Washington Mutual, Michael Goertz

What's Next for Retail
All photographs by Chris Eden
p. 200, La Encantada rendering by
Mike Burroughs

**PROJECTS**

Ayala Center Greenbelt
All photographs by Chris Eden

City Centre
All photographs by Chris Eden except
p. 20, p. 23, JF Housel
p. 21, bottom p. 24, Robert Pisano

Nordstrom
All photographs by Chris Eden

Grand Gateway
All photographs by Chris Eden

Suwon Gateway Plaza
All photographs by Chris Eden

Meydenbauer
p. 56, rendering by Scott Baumberger
p. 57, drawing by Callison

ACT Theatre
All photographs by Steve Keating
p. 61, drawing by Mike Burroughs

One Convention Place
All photographs by Chris Eden

Carillon Point
top p. 69, JF Housel
p. 70, Neil Rabinowitz

Gardenwalk
p.72, drawing by Callison
p.73, drawing by Scott Lockard

San Francisco Giants
All photographs by Chris Eden

W Hotel
All photographs by Chris Eden except
p. 85, Joe Mentele

Metropolitan Tower
All photographs by Chris Eden except
p. 90, JF Housel

Providence Health System
All photographs by Chris Eden except
p. 94, p.96-97, Chris Arend
p. 100-101, Steve Keating

St. Charles Medical Center
All photographs by Chris Eden

St. Francis Hospital Outpatient Center
All photographs by Chris Eden

Boeing Imax Theater and
Ackerley Family Exhibit Gallery
All photographs by Chris Eden

Pacific Science Center
All photographs by Dick Busher

Westin Westminster
All photographs by Chris Eden except
p. 123, p. 124-125, Mark Knight

Teton Club
All photographs by Chris Eden

The Inn at Semiahmoo
All photographs by Dick Busher

Village at Mammoth
All photographs by Chris Eden

Microsoft
All photographs by Chris Eden except
p. 145, JF Housel
p. 149, Fred Lichct

Eddie Bauer Corporate Headquarters
All photographs by Chris Eden except
p. 150, p. 153, Tim Hursley
p. 155, Ann Hopping

Future@Work
All photographs by Chris Eden

Latham & Watkins
All photographs by Chris Eden

SoftImage
All photographs by Paul Bielenberg

Orrick, Herrington & Sutcliffe, LLP
All photographs by Chris Eden

Boeing Customer Service Training Center
p. 172-173, 175, Fred Licht
p. 174 top left, John Gussman
p. 174 bottom, Ann Hopping

Boeing Company World Headquarters
All photographs by Chris Eden except
p. 183 bottom, p.184, pp. 186-187,
Craig Dugan©Hedrich Blessing

Cingular Wireless
All photographs by Chris Eden

FedEx World Service Centers
Renderings by Callison

FlatIron Crossing
All photographs by Chris Eden

Nike Goddess
All photographs by Chris Eden except
p. 214, p. 215 bottom, p.218 top right, p. 219,
Craig Dugan ©Hedrich Blessing

Ala Moana Center
All photographs by Chris Eden

Scottsdale Fashion Square
All photographs by Chris Eden

South Coast Plaza West
All photographs by Chris Eden

Jordan Creek Town Center
Renderings by Tim Ma Illustrations

Space Needle Pavilion
All photographs by Chris Eden

Harrods White Hall
All photographs by David Perks
courtesy of Harrods LTD.

Deira City Centre
All photographs by Reinhard Westphal

Seibu Department Store
All photographs by Chris Eden except
p. 252-253, Joel Riehl

**GLOBAL OPPORTUNITIES**

All drawings and renderings by
Callison Architecture except
p. 257, Emirates Experience, p. 258, Creek Landing,
p. 259, Continent Centre, Nawras Villas, and
Earth Isle by Scott Lockard
p. 259, The Gardens by Mike Burroughs and
Callison Architecture
p. 262, Aijian Shopping Center, Central Avenue, and
p. 264, New Century Square by Tim Ma
Illustrations and Wimberly Allison Tong & Goo
p. 264, Zhong Guan Cun by Beijing Yuan Jing
Architecture Illustration Co. and Tim Ma
Illustrations
p. 265, No. 1 Department Store by Tian Hua
Architecture Planning & Engineering Limited

**CHRONOLOGY**

All photographs by Chris Eden except
p. 266, Park Place by Dick Busher
p. 266, Koll Centre by JF Housel
p. 266, GTE Northwest Headquarters
by Robert Pisano
p. 267, Argent Hotel by John Sutton
p. 267, Seattle Repertory Theatre
by Steve Keating
p. 268, LL Bean by Maxwell Mackenzie

Every effort has been made to properly
credit individuals responsible for images in
this book.

Shawne Lewis   John C. Liles   William C. Liley   Renee Lillie   David P. Lindsey   Jennifer Little   Catherine Liuzzi   D

Andre Loewen   Eric Lofgran   Craig Lofgreen   Stephanie D. Long   Janet Longenecker   Stanley Lonseth   Irene Look   B

Nora Luehmann   Richard Lundstrom   Colleen Luque   Suzanne Lusnia   Patrick Lynch   Christina Lyons   Tianyi Tim M

Bethany Madsen   Chiho Maekawa   Mel Maertz   Carolyn Mahan   James N. Maiocco   Paul R. Makowicki   Jelena Maler

Andrea R. Marbet   Arthur Marcus   Joseph Marek   Matthew Marek   Anne Maresh   Sally Margolis   Debbie Marlow   Re

Darrell Mason   John A. Mason   Naomi Mason   William Massey   Jayne Matsudaira   Glen Matsui   Gary Matsumoto   Ma

Sheila E. May   Robert F. Maylan   Kristan Maynard   Virginia Maynard   Margaret Mazurkiewicz   Charlotte McAlister

Andrew McCune   Greg J. McDonald   Neil McDonald   Goef McIntosh   Holly McKinley   William McKnight   Rita McManu

John J. McWilliams   Michael Medina   Nichole Meehan   Ryan Meeks   Samantha Meinders   Halliday Nesiburger   Eduardo

Adam Merkl   Samantha Merrill   Asmellash Mesghinna   Christopher Metzger   Thomas Metzger   Walter Metzger   C. Ri

Dennis Mikkelsen   Steven Mikkelsen   Teresa Mikkola   Lisa Miller   Mark J. Miller   Richard Miller   Don Mills   Tatjana Mi

Robin Miwa   James Miyasato   Brian F. Moe   Robert Mohr   Chris Molinsky   Diane Monroe   Paul Moody   Steven W.

Morin   Melissa Morrier-Turk   Kimberly S. Morris   Elizabeth Morrisey   David Morton   Nancy Morton   Susan Morton   Th

Kelley Mullikin   Carsten Mullin   Rosalie Mullin   Gayle Mulliner   Mark Mullis   Ferdinand Munar   Chris Munro   M.

Monique Nailon   Ryan S. Najares   Kirk Nakahira   James Nakamoto   Patrick Nakamura   Elisabeth Nason   Julie Natsis

Charlene Nelson   Sheila Ness   Lisa Newland   Donald F. Newman   Desmond Ngai   Chuan T. Nguyen   Ming Nguye

Susanna L. Nielsen   Ronald Niemi   Christine Nightingale   James C. Norman   Arlene Nornes   Neidra North   Alex

Sarah Ocasek   Brian Ochs   Anneka O'Connell   John Odell   Charles O'Hern   Margie O'Keefe   David Okula   Erik Oldham

Kelly O'Neil   Terrance O'Neil   Bahareh Oreizy   Karen Oshiro   Kathleen Oshiro   Sigrid Ostlund   Michele Otake   Ros

Song-Kun Pak   Stanley Palmer   Tiffany Palmer   Sukyee Pang   Krisinda Parcel   Andrea Park   David Parker   J. Andrew

Julia Payne   Lisa Payne   J. Mack Pearl   Amy Pearson   Keith Pegorsch   Julie Pel   Cheri Pentilla   Zivko Penzar   Nora Pe

Connie J. Petersen   Lisbeth Petersen   Michael A. Petersen   Brian C. Peterson   Erik Peterson   Judy E. Peterson

Pflughoeft-Stewart   Dung M. Pham   Ryan R. Phelps   Diana Philbeck   Richard Phillippe   David Phillips   James P.

Bradford Potestio   Bridget Potter   Stefanie M. Powell   S. Ram Prasad   Robert Prendergast   Jeff Price   Michael P

Christopher Quinn   Robert Raasch   Deidre Raben   Steven Radkey   Steven Radomski   Kamini Raghavan   Ronald Raiche

Daniel Rasmussen   Linda Ray   David D. Read   Gilbert Recla   Gerald Redding   Gabriel D. Reed   Steven S. Reed   Angel

Jodi Richey   Rebecca Rickabaugh   Joel W. Riehl   Paul Ries   Michael Riggs   Peter Riley   Lynn Rinehart   Matthew

Corina Rodriguez   Kelly Rodriguez   Takao Rodriguez   Dennis Rogers   Linda Rogers   Stephen Romein   Jon Roney   B

Anne Russell   Colleen Rutten   Dick Rutter   David Ryan   Sara Sacra   Julianne Saeger   Fereidoun Saifnia   Michael Sai

Donna Sandstrom   Jennifer Saneholtz   Susan Sanford   Carolyn Sanscrainte   Melba Santos   Rene Sapper   Steve Sa

Karl Schmidt   Paul Schmidt   Elaine Schneider   Janelle Schneider   Douglas Schoemaker   Jeremy Schoenfeld   Skye Schro

Michael J. Scott   Michael P. Scott   David P. Scurlock   Stacy A. Scurlock   Seth Seablom   Naoto Sekiguchi   Cynthia Selkir

Catherine Sharp   Lori Sharp   Mark Sharp   Ben Sharpe   D. Douglas Shaw   Virgie Sheldon   Thadeaus Shelton   Williar

Todd Shumaker   Barry Shuman   Damian Sian   Denise Sico   Jackie Sideman   Shannon Sigler   Ivan Silantyev   Katy

James Skog   Bud Slater   Rodney Slater   Richard Sloniker   Gary Slotnik   Lynn Smalley   Petr Smidek   Andrew C. Sr

James Smotherman   Betsy Snell   H. Robert Soderstrom   Jeffrey Soehren   Ruth Sofer   Robert W. Sollinger   Stacy

Carl Stacy   David Staczek   Paula Stafford   Heather Staples   Jon Starwich   Sandra Staves   Stefan Stefansson   Den

Wendy Stone   John Stormont   Kelli Story   Laurie Straavaldson   W. Whitney Stretton   Linda Stroud   Candace Sugamu

Steve Swanson   Edward Sweetnam   Thomas Swoffer   John Swolgaard   David Syferd   David Tai   Daniel Taimanglo   Lind

John Taylor   Jonathan L. Taylor   Karen Taylor   Mark W. Taylor   William Taylor   Celeste Tell   Arthur Teller   Robert Tem

Mark Thometz   Carla Thompson   Janice Thompson   Linda J. Thompson   R. Allan Thunder   David Tilton   Lauren Tinda

Eric Trefcon   R. Patrick Trickler   Bruce Trimble   Vl Hien Troung   James Tubbs   Jon E. Tucker   Ted J. Udhus   Les

Katharine Van Anda   Peter Van Der Meulen   Sarah Van Eps   Jan Van Fossen   Kelly Van Gelder   Irene Van Nostrand

Barry Vaudrin   Athena Vaughan   Erin Vaughn   Stefanie Velasquez   Alexis Vera   Megan Verplank   Steve Viehmann   Jer

David Wakeford   James Waldowski   Ann Waldron   James D. Walker   Max R. Wall   Karen Wallace   Yu Wang   M.

Russell Watson   Brenda Watts   Carolyn Watts   Kimberly Weaver   Joseph Webber   Stephen Webster   Larry Weeks   Qingfe

Michael Whalen   Ronald Whatley   E. Anthony Wheeler   Patricia Whempner   June Whipple   Martha Whitaker   Alan D. Wh

George Wickwire   Teresa Wiesinger   Bret Wiggins   Grant Wilds   Echo Wiley   Caterine Wilkins   Kelsey Willard   Broc

Monica Wilson   Peter C. Wilson   Samuel R. Wilson   Tyler M. Wilson   Amy Wingate   Michael Winnick   Christina W

Theresa Wood   Roslyn Woodle   Tracy M. Woods   Linda Woodward   Michele Woodward   John Woolford   Doug Wrigh

Yan Yang   Teak Yap   Morris Yarnell   Sandra Yee   Se Hwa Yoo   Chad Yoshinobu   Mary Young   Sonia Yong   Shu Yin Yu   Tan Y